PETER THE GREAT

AND THE

OTTOMAN EMPIRE

BY

B. H. SUMNER

ARCHON BOOKS

HAMDEN, CONNECTICUT

1965

LIBRARY OF CONGRESS CATALOG CARD NUMBER: 65-10973
PRINTED IN THE UNITED STATES OF AMERICA

CONTENTS

Note.—All dates are given in the New Style, except where otherwise indicated.

I

THE GENERAL SETTING

DURING the half-century of Peter the Great's lifetime (1672—1725), Russia emerged, Austria triumphed, Turkey declined—but from a high point. Poland, despite John Sobieski, was rent. Venice, despite Morosini, sank further. In Persia the Safavi dynasty collapsed.

The Russian lunges against the Ottoman empire present a curious comparison with the Austrian achievements. After 1700 Charles XII and the Great Northern War prevented Peter from southward expansion. His capitulation on the Pruth even deprived him of what he had gained from the Sultan eleven years before in 1700. Only after Nystad was he able to recoup himself along the Caspian, and then more at the expense of Persia than of Turkey. Russia in the throes of feverish reorganization was not strong enough to move forward with success against both Sweden and Turkey at one and the same time; somewhat as under Ivan the Terrible she was not strong enough to cope with both Sweden and Poland combined. Then, however, she failed against both: under Peter she signally succeeded against Sweden. The Habsburgs, on the other hand, contrived to make head against Bourbons and Ottomans alike. Allies helped them greatly it is true, whereas effective allies in the main were lacking to Russia.

The contrast is indeed striking between 1683, when Kara Mustafa, the great Mehmed Koprili's son-in-law, was at the gates of Vienna, and 1718, when Prince Eugène's renewed victories compelled the signature of the treaty of Passarowitz. Thereby the Turks ceded not only the Banat, their last foothold north of the Danube in Hungary. Belgrade, captured for the second time within thirty years by the Austrians, was retained by them, and in addition Serbia and Little Wallachia. This was the high water-mark of Habsburg advance against the Ottomans for a hundred and fifty years and more. Except for the Bukovina (1775), no territorial gains were made from the Ottomans until 1878, when the administration of Bosnia and Herzegovina was taken over. Nor indeed was the high water-mark of 1718 maintained for long. The Emperor Charles VI, who had begun his reign with such striking successes against Louis XIV and Achmet III, closed it with the breakdown of the Pragmatic Sanction and the treaty of Belgrade (1739). Serbia, including Belgrade, and Little Wallachia once again became part of the Ottoman dominions.

Charles's father, Leopold I, in his eventful reign of forty-seven years (1658—1705), despite the ever-increasing menace of France, had been successful not merely in withstanding the Koprili revival of Ottoman power, but in passing over to the offensive. He had a triad of allies, Poland, Venice, and for the first time the new-comer Russia, as yet of little direct help; and he had a triad of remarkable military leaders, the Duke of Lorraine, the Marquis of Baden, Prince Eugène of Savoy. It is typical of the Habsburg empire—almost as polyglot as the Romanov or Ottoman empires—that none of these commanders were Austrians. Leopold's successes against the Turks were all the more telling in that the basic policies of the Habsburgs, notably in foreign affairs, were as usual immensely complicated by his dual position as Holy Roman Emperor and head of the Habsburg house. The process of trying to form a centralized administration in the Habsburg dominions was exceedingly slow and frequently interrupted, in contrast with the relatively rapid growth of central power in Muscovy. Although in the seventeenth century the Privy Council begins to be transformed from a primarily imperial into a primarily "Austrian" institution, the change had only begun, and Lobkowitz had failed in his experiment of transmuting the Privy Conference from a merely advisory council of ministers into an effective executive organ headed by something like a prime minister.[1] Sustained action in any field, particularly in foreign and military affairs, was slow and difficult. Throughout Leopold's reign the France of Louis XIV, the best organized power in Europe with the most proficient military technique, was an

[1] H. F. Schwarz, *The Imperial Privy Council in the Seventeenth Century* (Harvard; 1943), v-vi, 13, 187-189.

unremitting challenge to the Habsburg empire. Yet it was during this same period that Leopold was successful in gaining almost the whole of Hungary and Transylvania. But for the War of the Spanish Succession Peterwardein might have followed Zenta in less than twenty years. Not for nothing did the Turks have a great respect for Austrian power, in contrast with their belittlement of Russian military skill.[1]

The Austrians, for their part, won the treaties of Karlowitz and Passarowitz only after much hard fighting and a series of campaigns in the course of which they suffered a number of defeats. The Ottomans in the second half of the seventeenth century were a much tougher problem than in the first half. While the Austrians were absorbed in the West in the Thirty Years' War, the Ottoman empire, save under the brief rule of the energetic Murad IV (1632-40), had been a prey to incapable sultans, harem and Janissary intrigue, revolutions and bouts of anarchy. The first two Koprili grand viziers (1656—1676) harked back to the traditions of the great conquering sultans, and they effected a significant revival of Moslem power, as Venice, Poland and Vienna knew to their cost. So too did the governing oligarchy of palace courtiers in Constantinople, the successors of the slave family. Only extreme necessity had compelled them to call upon Mehmed Koprili to become grand vizier. It took them many years before they could regain secure control of affairs from that able Albanian family.[2] By the time Peter the Great took the reins of government into his own capacious hands (1695), "the men of the pen", the palace functionaries with regular access to the sultan, and the *ulema* were in the ascendancy. After Hussein, the last effective Koprili grand vizier (1698—1702), there was no strong successor, and for the next sixteen years Constantinople was a prey to political vicissitudes of exceptional rapidity and complexity. "Three things are lacking to-day in this empire:

---

[1] Report of Tolstoi, 1703, in Russian foreign office archives, paraphrased by T. K. Krylova, 'Russko-turetskie otnosheniya vo vremya severnoi voiny', in *Istoricheskie Zapiski*, 1941, x, 255. Tolstoi added however that Constantinople was much perturbed by reports as to the reorganization of the Russian army and particularly by the building of a fleet in the Sea of Azov.

[2] W. L. Wright, *Ottoman Statecraft* ... (Princeton; 1935), 58-9.

intelligence, single-mindedness, and money". Such was the verdict at this time (1705) of the very experienced patriarch of Jerusalem, chief political informant of the Russian ambassador.[1] Russian diplomacy, new to the Bosphorus, was taxed to the uttermost by the palace kaleidoscope, but had the Sultan enjoyed a stable and consecutive government Russia might have fared worse than she did.

On "the ever-victorious frontier" there was ever less success, in Europe at any rate. A wise Turkish counsellor, Said Mehmed Pasha, wrote about this time: "Let the Janissaries . . . be well disciplined, few but élite, and all present in time of need."[2] By the early eighteenth century the exact contrary was in fact the case. The first two Koprilis had disciplined and reinspired the army, largely by providing it with regular and ample pay. But the revival had not been maintained, even though the increasing use of Albanians and Bosnians provided an admirable toughening of the army. It is true that the janissaries were spasmodically capable of formidable, militant energy against the infidel, but for the most part their army duties were badly neglected. They cherished their immunities, not their duties, and they effectively prevented any thorough-going reform of the army.[3] They had long since ceased to be recruited from Christian tribute boys,[4] and had become a privileged, married, hereditary caste, recruited from and closely linked with the Moslem population. Thus they had become the exact opposite of what had been originally intended—and effected—when this military order had been instituted. The janissaries had indeed become not unlike the *streltsy*, though earlier they had nothing in common with these Muscovite praetorian guards. They differed however in one essential respect. No sultan was able to reform them effectively, still less to abolish them, until Mahmud II destroyed them in

---

[1] N. Th. Kapterev, *Snosheniya Ierusalimskikh Patriarkhov s russkim pravitelstvom*, in *Pravlosavny Palestinsky Sbornik*, 1895, xv, pt. 1, 342 (cited hereafter as *Snosheniya..*).

[2] W. L. Wright, *op. cit.*, 99.

[3] W. L. Wright, *op. cit.*, 45.

[4] The law for collecting Christian tribute boys remained nominally in force until 1750, but the last recorded instance of its enforcement is in 1637: *ib.*, 39. According to N. Jorga, *Geschichte des osmanischen Reiches*, iv (Gotha; 1911), 158, the last recorded instance is 1663.

1826. That was one hundred and twenty-eight years after Peter the Great had crushed the *streltsy* in blood and banishment.

As a boy of ten, Peter had witnessed the savage coup d'état of 1682 carried out by means of the *streltsy*, who had massacred his mother's supporters and installed his half-sister Sophia as regent. For him they were "in truth nothing but begetters of evil, and not soldiers."[1] By destroying them utterly, when they mutinied in 1698, he swept away at one and the same stroke the main obstacle to his army reorganization and the one armed nucleus of opposition to europeanization. His new guard regiments took the place of the *streltsy*. These were militarily up to date and efficient, trained on the European model, and they were politically imbued with belief in Peter's aims. The Russian guards, initially recruited almost solely from landowners and country squires, played a decisive part in politics and administration throughout the eighteenth century, and they made or unmade every Russian sovereign, on accession or deposition, for a hundred years after Peter's death. But throughout the century they looked to the West. They were not the myrmidons of nationalist or religious reaction as were the janissaries.

The Ottoman armies and the Ottoman state needed reform. In the early eighteenth century there was, indeed, a notable change in the structure and the spirit of important elements among the governing class of the Empire. In particular, more and more influence was exercised by the Kalemaschis or Effendis, some Moslem, some Greek, the new type of "men of the pen".[2] As the Greeks of the Phanar were to show so conspicuously throughout the century, the tangled reins of government and of diplomacy were seldom effectively held by the old type of "men of the sword". To some extent, above all in the army and navy,

[1] *Pisma i Bumagi Petra Velikago*, i, 381, text of letter of Peter to Dositheus, patriarch of Jerusalem, 15 August, 1700.

[2] Lady Mary Wortley-Montague did not greatly exaggerate when she wrote (Letter xxvii): "They (the effendis) are the only men really considerable in the Empire, all the profitable employments and church revenues are in their hands . . . You may easily judge of the power of these men, who have engrossed all the wealth of the Empire. 'Tis they who are the real authors, tho' the soldiers are the actors of revolutions." She was less near the mark, as well as inconsistent, when in the next letter she wrote: "The government here is entirely in the hands of the army. The Grand Vizier, with all his absolute power, . . . trembles at a Janizary's frown."

European technical skill was required. Something was done by a long series of French instructors and by renegades from Italy, Poland, Hungary, or elsewhere. But nothing that was done was for a moment comparable with the effect of Peter the Great on Russia. Though he failed to recoup himself for the disaster on the Pruth, he set Russia on a path which was to assure her of ultimate superiority over Turkey.

To compare with Peter no sultan arose. In Constantinople, power was bandied about between the "men of the pen", the tentacular bureaucrats, the scions of the palace school, the seraglio, "the men of the sword", and the *ulema*, with the janissaries to be humoured or bought and the city mob to be assuaged. The sultans themselves no longer really governed, and at this time few could even die on the throne. Mohammed IV, "the hunter", who began his reign at the age of seven in 1649, ended it in deposition in 1687. His two sons, both of them pitted against Peter, ended likewise, Mustafa II in 1703, Achmet III, "the miser", in 1730. The janissary rebellion and palace revolution of 1703, which removed Mustafa, were the obverse to the rebellion and crushing of the *streltsy* five years earlier.[1] Muscovy moved forward through holocausts: Turkey gyrated fruitlessly in holocausts.

The political weaknesses of the Ottoman empire appear all too evident, especially in the eyes of Western historians, but the study of the Ottoman administration from Turkish sources has as yet hardly begun. In the coming years much will probably be altered in the indiscriminate picture usually painted of the decadence of the Ottoman empire at the beginning of the eighteenth century. If the empire was crumbling, it was only crumbling on some of its fringes. If the organization of power in Constantinople was rotting, it was a slow rot. The bark of the great tree had not

---

[1] The 1703 rebellion not only resulted in the deposition of the sultan, which was nothing new in Ottoman annals, but in an unprecedented event, never repeated. The new mufti issued a firman for the execution of his predecessor, the redoubtable but rapacious reformer, Feizullah, and the execution was carried out, with every possible public indignity. Hammer-Purgstall, *Histoire de l'empire ottoman* . . . (Paris; 1839), xiii, 132-3; Jorga, *op. cit.*, iv, 289. Sutton, the English minister at Constantinople, reported, 23 Sept. (O.S.), 1703, that the mufti was "abandoned to the rages of the soldiery, who in the most ignominious manner, cut off and exposed his head and pudenda". Public Record Office (P.R.O.), State Papers (S.P.), 97/21.

been ringed. The Anatolian sap still rose, even if with increasing difficulty. Westerners are apt to think too much in terms of Turkey in Europe, to forget Turkey in Africa, to forget the essential Turkey in Asia. Only three pashaliks carried with them the coveted right to "three tails": only one of these was in Europe, Buda: the other two were Baghdad and Cairo.[1]

Although Ottoman power was giving ground on the Danube, it was on the increase in the Caucasus from the time of the Georgian campaigns of 1703-4, even before the final collapse of the Safavi dynasty in Persia pitted Turkey, Persia, and Russia against each other for control of the Caucasus and the western Caspian. Westerners tend to fasten their eyes on the Balkan Christians. The Russians of Peter the Great's time had indeed large eyes for them, but they were also becoming almost equally aware of the fact that the far-spreading, polyglot, but dominantly Moslem empire of the Ottomans included, or was threatening to include, the Trans-Caucasian Christians. Peter's relations with Georgian refugees and the Georgian principalities and with the Armenians fall outside the limits of this study, but their significance and the lively distrust they aroused in Constantinople must not be minimized. Though it did not then come to actual war with Turkey, Peter's conquest from Persia of her Caspian provinces at the end of his reign rang up the curtain on the three-cornered struggle for the North Caucasus steppes and the Trans-Caucasia, a struggle in which the Georgians and Armenians played something of the same role as the Serbs and Bulgars in European Turkey.

In Peter's day, for both the Balkan and the Trans-Caucasian Christians Russia was too far away for sustained intervention. She lay beyond the steppes of the Black Sea littoral and the Kuban. These were still the abode of Tatar peoples, Moslems, owing subordination to Turkey, who held key fortresses on the coast with garrisons of her own. Of these peoples, the most developed and the most important were the Crimean Tatars, now much more closely tied to Constantinople than heretofore. For two centuries and more the Crimean vassal khanate had been a major issue in

[1] Jorga, *op. cit.*, iv, 171.

Russian foreign relations. Still with Peter, as before, Russian relations with Turkey hinged above all on the Crimea and the Black Sea steppes.

The Crimean khanate, though declining in power and rent by internal dissensions, was still a dangerous menace to Russia's steady expansion southwards. It was an essential factor in the struggle for the control of the right-bank Dnieper and the Zaporozhian Cossacks. This struggle, to which Peter was heir, remained undecided by him. But by the time he died in 1725 the balance was tilting against the Crimea; even after the catastrophe on the Pruth, the Tatars were unable to secure from Peter any admission of tribute to the khan. The Turks kept an increasingly firm hand on their vassal, and the khan and his principal officers were appointed and removed by the Sultan, who relied on the Tatar cavalry as much as ever in his campaigns against the Austrians, as well as of course against the Poles and the Russians. Throughout Peter's lifetime, and beyond it, the khanate was almost continuously in the hands of Selim-Girei and five alternating sons of his. Selim-Girei himself—poet and historian as well as warrior[1]—stands out as one of the most remarkable of the nine great khans lauded by Crimean chroniclers. He was doubly unique in being invested no less than four times as khan, and in being the only khan to make the Mecca pilgrimage. One of his sons, the unruly Devlet-Girei, three times khan, the khan of Poltava and the Pruth, was also numbered among the nine. He ranks conspicuously as the inveterate foe of the Russians, a fierce fighter—against all comers, including his brothers—and a most dangerous intriguer in Constantinople. There he worked his hardest for war on the northern front against the peace party and against those who aimed at the reconquest of the Morea and the renewal of the struggle against the Austrians and belittled the urgency of the Russian menace to the Crimea.[2]

[1] Hammer-Purgstall, *Geschichte der Chane der Krim* (Vienna; 1856), 185, using Crimean sources. K. D. Smirnov, *Krymskoe Khanstvo* . . . (St. Petersburg; 1887), 710, also using Crimean sources, states that this is unsubstantiated, but that he certainly was a lover of poetry and history.

[2] In the space of sixty-eight years, from 1671 to 1739, there were twelve different khans. Selim-Girei and five of his sons account for six of these (marked with *). From 1671, when Selim-Girei was first made khan, until his death in 1705 he reigned

II

THE CRIMEA, AZOV AND THE BLACK SEA

PETER THE GREAT inherited two main problems in the South—the Crimean Tatars and the Cossacks. They were closely interlinked and they involved both Turkey and Poland. As always in Russo-Turkish relations Poland played a major part. Peter inherited a policy of alliance with Poland, since 1686, against Turkey. Poland for her part was also allied with Austria and Venice against Turkey, and was engaged in the struggle for

during twenty-two years. From 1692 to 1739 the khanate was continuously held by him and his line, save for a few months. The following list is based on Smirnov, Hammer-Purgstall and H. H. Howorth, *History of the Mougols* (London; 1880), pt. ii. The appointment of a khan was for seven years.

*1. Selim-Girei, May 1671—Feb. 1678. Deposed after Chigirin.
 2. Murad-Girei, 1678—1683: cousin of 1. Deposed after siege of Vienna: died 1695.
 3. Hadschi-Girei, Oct. 1683—June 1684: first cousin of 2.
*4. Selim-Girei, June 1684—1691: second time: resigned to go on pilgrimage to Mecca.
 5. Seadet-Girei, March 1691—Dec. 1691: nephew of 1.
 6. Safa-Girei, Jan. 1692—Oct. 1692: had been *kalga* under Murad-Girei at siege of Vienna.
*7. Selim-Girei, 1692—March 1699: third time: resigned.
*8. Devlet-Girei, March 1699—Dec. 1702: son of 1. Deposed for false information against Russians.
*9. Selim-Girei, Dec. 1702—Dec. 1704: fourth time: resigned; he died in 1705, well over seventy and racked by gout.
*10. Kazi-Girei, 1705—April, 1707: son of 1: had been *kalga* of 9: deposed and died soon after.
*11. Kaplan-Girei, 1707—Dec. 1707: son of 1: deposed for defeat by a Circassian confederacy and assistance to fugitive Don Cossacks during Bulavin's revolt.
*12. Devlet-Girei, Dec. 1707—March 1713: second time.
*13. Kaplan-Girei, 1713—1716: second time: deposed for failing to be present at Peterwardein.
*14. Devlet-Girei, 1716—Dec. 1716: third time.
 15. Kara Devlet-Girei: deposed after a few days.
*16. Seadet-Girei, 1717—Oct. 1724: son of 1.
*17. Mengli-Girei, 1724—Oct. 1730: son of 1.
*18. Kaplan-Girei, 1730—Sept. 1736: third time. Deposed after Lacey's first devastation of the Crimea.
 19. Feth-Girei, 1736—July, 1737; son of 14.
*20. Mengli-Girei, 1737-39: second time. Died 1739, after peace of Belgrade.

the Polish lands between the Dniester and the Dnieper that swayed to and fro ever since the Turks in 1672 had decided on a northward drive to seize the Polish Ukraine. The division of the Ukraine in 1667 between Muscovy and Poland had given to the former Ukraine on the left bank of the Dnieper, together with Kiev itself and a small rayon, and to the latter Ukraine on the right bank of the Dnieper. But both Russia and Poland remained cut off from the Black Sea by a broad, fluctuating belt of steppe land, stretching from southern Bessarabia (the Budjak) right round to the mouth of the Don, where the strong Turkish fortress of Azov barred the access of the Don Cossacks to the Sea of Azov. These treeless pampas were the grazing grounds of the Crimean Tatars and their tributaries, the half dozen loose-knit hordes of the Nogais. Near the Dnieper cataracts lay the Sech, the stronghold of the redoubtable Zaporozhian Cossacks, playing for their own free hands now with Muscovy, now with Poland, now with the Crimea, now with Turkey direct; grazing, fishing, and hunting on both banks and going for salt down to the mouth of the Dnieper.

Those Cossacks who were left to Poland on the right bank of the Dnieper for long harboured the idea of restoring the briefly united Ukraine of Bohdan Khmelnitsky, with the aid either of the Russians or of the Turks and the Crimea. The same hope had supporters in the Russian Ukraine, but not if a united Ukraine was to be won only at the price of the Uniate religion or a vassal Ukraine under Turkish suzerainty, like Moldavia or Wallachia. The appeal of Orthodoxy told heavily against Moslem and Catholic alike. In 1676 direct war over these right-bank Ukrainian lands was waged between Muscovy and Turkey, the first such war save for the Turkish Astrakhan campaign more than a century before (1569-70).[1] In it a major part was played by the Tatars, and the indeterminate peace which patched up an in-

---

[1] See P. A. Sadikov, "Pokhod Tatar i Turok na Astrakhan v 1569 g.", in *Istoricheskie Zapiski*, 1947, xxii, 132-66, printing for the first time in full Maltsev's report; H. Inalchik, *The Origin of the Ottoman-Russian rivalry and the Don-Volga canal (1569)* (Ankara, 1948; in English as well as Turkish); N. A. Smirnov, *Rossiya i Turtsiya v xvi-xvii vv.* (Moscow; 1946), i, 89-125; A. N. Novoselsky, *Borba moskovkago gosvdartsva statarimi* . . . (Moscow; 1948), 24-28.

decisive war, that had been equally costly and disturbing to both sides, was initially concluded at Bakhchi-Sarai, the khan's residence in the Crimea (1681).[1]

Within six years Muscovy attempted an invasion of the Crimea itself, for the first time in her annals. In 1686 Poland finally agreed to the permanent cession of Kiev to Muscovy, but in return Muscovy had to enter into an offensive alliance against Turkey. Golitsyn's army marched right across the open steppes to the isthmus of Perekop (1687), some three hundred miles from the Muscovite confines, but the expedition was ruined by mismanagement and lack of water and supplies. Golitsyn repeated his campaign two years later, with still more lamentable results.[2] For two centuries Muscovy had had three major scores against the Crimean Tatars, the toll of raids,[3] the toll of prisoners (sold in

[1] For the negotiations and peace of Bakhchi-Sarai, see Soloviev, *Istoriya Rossii* ... (3rd ed.), xiii, 849-56, and N. A. Smirnov, *op. cit.* ii, 165-68. An Italian text of the twelve articles accepted by the Sultan is given in Hammer-Purgstall, *op. cit.* xii, 502-4. He did not accept an article acknowledging the Zaparozhian Cossacks to be under Russian control.

[2] At the time of Golitsyn's Crimean campaigns demands were put forward of so fantastic a character that they can only be treated as defiant fanfaronade (Bogoslovsky, *Petr I* (Moscow, 1940-48), i, 207): the Crimea, Ochakov, Azov, and the mouth of the Don were to be ceded to Russia: the Tatars were to be removed from the Crimea and resettled in Anatolia: all Russian prisoners in the Crimea and in Turkey were to be handed back without ransom: a large war indemnity was to be paid. Such claims were not realized until a century later under Catherine the Great. They were never repeated until Osterman put forward even wider proposals in the instructions he drew up for himself for the Nemitov conference of 1737; A. A. Kochubinsky, *Graf Osterman i razdyel Turtsii* (Odessa; 1889), 211-21, 236-39.

[3] During Peter's lifetime the raids of the Crimean Tatars (occasionally as in 1713 assisted by the Kuban Tatars) seem to have been more severe than during the reign of his father Alexis. This can be accounted for by the fact that Russia and Turkey were three times at war with one another, 1676-81, 1687-99, 1710-13, and to the fact that Slobodskaya Ukraine, which was now Russian and filling up rapidly, lay to the south of the well fortified Byelgorod line and was less distant from the Crimea. As previously, the usual raids were in small parties of not more than one or two hundred, but in the great raids the Tatars were said to have numbered as many as 15,000 (1693); and even 30,000 (1713). The most damaging of the widespread raids, apart from those on the right-bank Ukraine, were those of 1680 (led by the khan in person), 1691, 1713 and 1717. The following figures give an indication of their seriousness: 1680, 3,014 killed and prisoners, 21,770 head of stock driven off; 1691, 1,962 prisoners, 85 killed, 4,902 head of stock driven off; 1713, 14,340 prisoners; 1717, 712 killed, 10,600 prisoners, 163,000 head of stock driven off. D. I. Bagalyei, *Ocherki iz istorii kolonizatsii stepnoi okrainy* ... (Moscow; 1887) 254, 295, 460-67; and his *Istoriya Slobodskoi Ukraini* (Kharkov; 1918), 53-6, and *Ocherki iz russkoi istorii* (Kharkov; 1913), ii, 4; *Sbornik imp. russkago istoricheskago obshchestva* (cited hereafter as *Sbornik* ...), xxv, 345-48 (1712), 373-75 (1713);.

the Turkish slave markets or held to ransom)[1], and the toll of
annual tribute to the khan, disguised as 'gifts'. Now, in addition,
Peter had two major disasters to avenge. For five years after the
costly failure of 1689 nothing of consequence was attempted.

Golikov, *Dyeyaniniya Petra Velikago* (Moscow; 1788-97), xi supplement, 498—500
(1717). These were exceptionally successful raids, and the figures given, particularly for 1713 and 1717, should be accepted with reserve. Unfortunately, for this
period there is nothing corresponding with A. A. Novoselsky's admirable, detailed
study, *Borba moskovskago gosudarstva s tatarimi v pervoi polovinye xvii v.* (Moscow;
1948).

   The great raid of 1717 was directed mainly up the Volga and penetrated as far
as the outskirts of Saratov, Penza and Voronezh. That of 1711 was primarily
directed against the Voronezh shipyards, though it failed of its objective and was
turned back with comparatively little loss. But the great majority of the raids fell
upon Slobodskaya Ukraine, the region of the Donets with Kharkov as its chief
centre. Though colonised almost entirely by Ukrainians both from the Russian
left bank Ukraine and from the right bank Ukraine, it was under the authority not
of Mazepa or his successor Samoilovich but of Moscow; but it was largely autonomous and its defence measures were none too well co-ordinated. After the middle
of the seventeenth century, when the elaborate Byelgorod defence line was constructed, nothing on such a scale was attempted further south to cover the new
settlements that were very rapidly forming Slobodskaya Ukraine. These were
originally organized in frontier regiments, but during Peter's reign the country was
also filling up with ordinary farmers and traders. It was both the nearest and the
most lucrative region for Tatar raids.

   In Feodor's reign a new defence line was constructed to guard the colonies of the
previous twenty-five years, but it was much less elaborate and less efficiently organized than the Byelgorod line had been, and the southward expansion of "the
frontier" during Peter's reign rendered the new line to a considerable extent out of
date (Bagalyei, *Ocherki iz istorii kolonizatsii . . .*, 481-90). Peter, like V. V. Golitsyn,
believed in taking the offensive as the right policy against so mobile a foe as the
Tatars, whose object was booty not battle or the capture of fortified places. Hence
he took no steps to extend the old type of defence line, though it is true that projects
for so doing were mooted. In fact the enormous drafts that he made on Ukrainian
manpower were used (apart from the army) on the Voronezh shipyards and on the
building of St. Petersburg. It was not until the reign of the Empress Anna that
Ukrainians were set to work (1730-34) to the direct advantage of their own land
on the construction of "the Ukrainian line", which linked the Donets with the
Dnieper (Bagalyei, *op. cit.*, 295—312).

[1] The ransoming of prisoners was so regular and important a burden that there
was a special tax levied for the purpose, the *polonyanichniya dengi*, and a special
department existed to deal with it. For a few years (1667-72) there was even an
independent *polonyanichny prikaz*, not under the foreign office or any other department: A. Lappo-Danilevsky, *Organizatsiya pryamago oblozheniya v moskovskom
gosudarstvye . . .* (St. Petersburg; 1890), 477-78; S. A. Byelokurov, *O posolskom
prikazye* (Moscow; 1906), 40-41; S. K. Bogoyavlensky, *Prikaznye sudi XVII vyeka*
(Moscow; 1946), 119; D. I. Bagalyei, *Ocherki iz kolonizatsii . . .*, 266-68. Of course
not all the prisoners were taken by the Crimean Tatars, but their share was very
large, and on occasion exceptionally valuable. In 1660 the leader of one of the
greatest families in Muscovy fell into their hands, Vasily Borisovich Sheremeteyev:
2,000 Tatar prisoners were said to have been offered in exchange for him; Hurmuzaki, *Fragmente zur Geschichte der Rumanen* (Bucarest; 1885), iii, 271, citing an

Meanwhile, Petrik, a Cossack renegade from hetman Mazepa, was working actively with the Tatars and the Turks, in the role of a second Doroshenko, to rouse the Zaparozhian Cossacks to sweep north and reunite the Ukraine under Moslem protection. He failed to win over any but a minority in the Sech, and accomplished nothing effectual. But Mazepa, and to a lesser extent Moscow, were uneasy. A southward drive would mend matters.

At the same time the Muscovite government was under increasingly heavy pressure from their nominal allies the Poles and from the Austrians to aid them by action against Turkey. Appeals for help were intensified by the vehement and indefatigable agent of Moscow, Dositheus, patriarch of Jerusalem. His flighty and hectoring advice did not move Moscow to rapid action, but he struck home when he wrote with outspoken downrightness: "The Crimean Tatars are but a handful and they boast that they receive tribute from you. The Tatars are Turkish subjects, so it follows that you are Turkish subjects. Many times you have boasted that you will do such and such, but all finishes with words only, and nothing in fact is done."[1] Finally, in 1695 Peter resumed active hostilities. He did so, however, not by attempting another direct attack on the Crimea, but by the novel stroke of an attack on Azov.

Sixty years earlier the Don Cossacks had seized and held Azov for five years (1637—1642), thereby ensuring free exit from the Don. Muscovy had emphatically decided against supporting them. She would have no war with Turkey. When the Turks

Austrian report of 1668. Two thousand apparently were not enough; at any rate Sheremeteyev was kept prisoner until 1681.

The Russians were at a disadvantage in that they usually had far fewer Tatar prisoners than their enemy. In 1692 the Tatars mocked the Muscovite envoys: "In the Crimea we have a hundred and twenty thousand and more of the Muscovite and Cossack people, but in Moscow there are but two or three thousand of ours. How set free without ransom?" Soloviev, *op. cit.*, xiv, 1112. Whatever the real numbers, Peter was unable to secure in the treaty of Constantinople (1700) anything more than an involved and none too favourable article on exchange of prisoners and ransom of captives; Bogoslovsky, *op. cit.*, v, 212-15. After his disaster on the Pruth he could obtain nothing. In 1739 by the treaty of Belgrade the Russians were, on paper, extremely successful, gaining the exchange of "all prisoners and slaves made either before or during the war" of 1736-39: Noradounghian, *Recueil d'actes internationaux de l'empire ottoman* (Paris; 1897); i, 201, 261-2.

[1] Report from Dositheus, 28 March, 1691, received in Moscow September; extracts in Soloviev, *op. cit.*, xiv, 1145.

reconquered it, they fortified it strongly and made it the main bulwark against the Don Cossacks and their depredations by sea, as well as a main centre of their influence in.the Kuban steppes. From time to time, notably during the Chigirin war (1676-81), Muscovite troops had been sent to reinforce the Don Cossacks against expected Turkish attack. Once, in 1646, naval help of an ineffectual kind was sent.[1] But no major actions had occurred, and until Peter the Great Muscovy had not challenged Turkey at Azov.

Peter captured Azov at his second attempt, in 1696, thanks to his new fleet, Austrian engineers and unified command. When he made his first attempt the year before he had none of these. His troops had indeed, in large part, been transported by boats, down the Don and down the Volga to Tsaritsyn, but neither he nor the Don Cossacks had a war flotilla strong enough to prevent the Turkish fleet from bringing in reinforcements. This was the decisive fact that led Peter to his immensely costly shipbuilding programme at and near Voronezh, far up the Don, beyond probable reach of Tatar raids and near good forest supplies. It was not merely a powerful armed shallow-draft flotilla that he built, but sea-going men of war, ships of the line. Having captured Azov, he proceeded to found a naval station not far off at Taganrog, and to take even more than usually drastic steps to colonize and supply labour for his new acquisitions. A greatly enlarged building programme was laid down and was carried out, despite immense difficulties and many delays, under the technical supervision of Dutch, Italian and English masters, and with much recruitment of foreign seamen.[2] Already by the end of 1699 he

---

[1] The middle Volga towns were ordered to construct boats for despatch to the Don via the Tsaritsyn portage. 99 boats reached the Don, but they were either ramshackle or unsuitable for use at sea: N. A. Smirnov, *Rossiya i Turtsiya v XVI—XVII vv.* (Moscow; 1946), ii, 97, 99.

[2] One main object of Peter's "great embassy" to the West in 1697-98 was to hire shipwrights and seamen for his Azov fleet. He was very successful in so doing, even though he failed entirely in his major diplomatic aim of a war combination against Turkey and the hiring of a Dutch fleet and Dutch artillery. Foremost among the Dutchmen who took service under Peter at this time was Cruys, who served him as a leading naval expert and commander for the rest of his life. Both at this time and later Peter laid special emphasis on the recruitment of Slavs for his service, including the navy. Ostrovsky's mission in 1697 to "the Slavenian or

had at sea a fleet of fourteen ships of the line, the largest of
sixty-two guns, and he himself sailed with them to the straits of
Kerch, to demand passage to Constantinople for his envoy,
Ukraintsev, in the forty-six gun *Kryepost*.[1]

Azov opened the way only to the sea of that name. The narrow
straits of Kerch were the key to the entry into the Black Sea itself,
and it was necessary for Peter to secure them. He was aiming
to do so with his new fleet and with a revivified Holy Alliance.
In 1697 he concluded the first Russian alliance with Austria against
Turkey, but events in the West and the shadow of the Spanish
succession soon determined the Austrians to seek immediate
peace with the Turks. Peter's visit to Vienna (1698) failed to keep
Austria to her alliance. At the peace negotiations at Karlowitz
the Russian envoy, Voznitsyn, found himself virtually isolated:
the Austrians, Poles, Venetians made peace for themselves, while

Slovatskian and Sclavonian land" (in fact he did not get further than Venice) was
in part with the object of taking into Russian service sea-captains and navigators
from the Adriatic coast: text of Ostrovsky's instructions in *Pisma i Bumagi Petra
Velikago*, i, 656. Cruys in 1698 succeeded in recruiting 101 Slavs and Greeks almost
all of whom were sailors of various descriptions; Ustryalov, *Istoriya tsarstvovaniya
Petra Velikago*, iii, 576, 580, and S. Elagin, *Istoriya russkogo flota*; *prilozheniya* (St.
Petersburg; 1894), ii, 200-207; cf., Bogoslovsky, *op. cit.*, ii, 266-67, 333, for the recruiting of Slav sailors in 1697.

Tolstoi, after his arrival in Constantinople as Russian minister in 1702, was very
active in making connections with Slavs, Italians and Greeks from the Adriatic
coast lands, partly as sources of information, partly as recruits for the Russian navy.
Botsis (d. 1714) a Dalmatian Greek, originally a Turkish subject, but for a long spell
of years in the Venetian galley fleet, was one of Tolstoi's first acquisitions. He was
taken into the Olonet galley squadron in 1703 and was one of the makers of Peter's
Baltic galley fleet, rising to the rank of rear-admiral. Zmaevich (d. 1735), from
Cattaro, the younger brother of bishop Zmaevich (see below, p. 63), who had also
served in the Venetian galleys, was another recruit of Tolstoi. He was imprisoned
with him in Constantinople at the time of the Pruth campaign (1710-11), but succeeded in getting to Russia in 1712, played a conspicuous part in the Baltic galley
fleet and was made a vice-admiral. Peter's first galley commander, Lima, a Genoese,
who distinguished himself highly at the capture of Azov, was not a newcomer to
Russia. He had entered the Russian army under Feodor Alekseyevich. He returned
to the army after the second Azov campaign, did well at Narva, and was killed
the year after (1701).

[1] Bogoslovsky, *op. cit.*, iv, 56, 86. The *Kryepost* was one of ten ships built
on the lines of Barbary pirate ships, *ib.*, 53, and iii, 164. It may have added to the
disgust and shock of the Turks in Constantinople to see that this first Russian man
of war ever to sail on the Black Sea or enter the Golden Horn owed so much to
the Barbary corsairs, the nominal subjects of the sultan. Ukraintsev's reports on
his arrival in Constantinople and his negotiations are analysed in minute detail in
the fifth (and last) volume of Bogoslovsky, *Petr I.*

Voznitsyn could do no better than conclude a truce.[1] This was the origin of Peter's lasting animosity against the Habsburgs: they had deceived and abandoned him. He never forgot or forgave their treatment of him. Years later, he still fell into violent passion when talking of Karlowitz: they grossly misused him, "taking no more notice of him than a dog": "In my lifetime I shall never forget what they have done to me, I feel it, and am come off with empty pockets."[2]

Karlowitz destroyed any solid hope of obtaining Kerch. The Austrians had accepted the basis of *uti possidetis* for negotiations, which undermined in advance the Russian demands for the cession of Kerch. The demand was repeated by Ukraintsev, but equally without success. By then (1700) rapid peace with Turkey was essential. The northern alliance against Sweden had duly borne its fruit in war, and Peter was now intent on joining Augustus of Saxony against Charles XII. Peace with Turkey was so urgently required that Ukraintsev was even instructed to agree to the razing of the four Dnieper fortresses held by the Russians, the retention of which he had previously to insist on "without fail".[3]

These fortresses, below the cataracts in the great bend of the Dnieper, had been a special bone of contention. They were the fruit of a successful subsidiary attack launched in 1695 under Sheremeteyev down the Dnieper. The object had been, not to thrust forward in Galitsyn's ill-omened tracks to Perekop, but to divert Tatar forces from the Azov front, to endanger Crimean communications by land westward, and to strengthen Russian influence with the Zaporozhian Cossacks. Sheremeteyev was extremely successful. He captured in succession four Turkish

---

[1] A very detailed account of the Karlowitz negotiations from the Russian angle is now available in Bogoslovsky, *op. cit.*, iii, 345—454, cf. H. Uebersberger, *Russlands Orientpolik* . . . (Stuttgart; 1913), 61-64. Strangely enough Voznitsyn was initially left unprovided with written instructions. The confusion among the Russians in Vienna must have been very extreme owing to the news of the Streltsy revolt, Peter's immediate start for Moscow and the consequent abandonment of the visit to Venice which he was about to make.

[2] Reports of Whitworth to St. John 12 and 13 Oct. 1711, on audience with Peter: text in *Sbornik*, lxi, 2, 35.

[3] Bogoslovsky, *op. cit.*, iv, 69, 355; v, 119-31, 199-203, 206-9, 218-220, 239. "Without fail" was added by Golovin to Ukraintsev's original instructions. The four forts were Gazi-Kerman, Taman (Dugan), Nustretkermen, and Saginkermen.

fortified posts on the lower Dnieper, and held them against counter-attacks on a considerable scale. The Russian outposts were almost down to the Dnieper estuary, and they were establishing themselves solidly in their new fort of Kamenny Zaton, over against the Sech. The Crimean Tatars were quite as much, if not more, perturbed by this forward move down the Dnieper as by the offensive against Azov. The Russian successes not only hampered their raids and threatened their grazing and hunting grounds, but equally menaced their land communications across the Dnieper with the Nogais in Khanskaya Ukraine[1] and the Budzhak, and with the Turkish fortresses of Ochakov at the mouth of the Bug, and Akkerman (Belgorod), Bender and Hotin on the Dniester. Their regular routes for joining the Turkish armies in the field against Poland or Austria were now none too safe.

At the very time of Peter's 1695 campaign the Turks were pressing the khan hard for troops against the Austrians, and that summer Selim-Girei himself with a contingent was serving on the Danube near Widdin. Sheremeteyev's campaign created the utmost alarm. To the defence of Azov, far away to the east, the Tatars contributed but little, and when they did send reinforcements next year they did so belatedly and in driblets.[2] Nor after the capture of Azov did they make any move of their own for its recapture. They had not sufficient skill or strength. "For a Tatar there is nothing to do at a city: we are not townsfolk."[3] Such had been the Tatar remonstrance to the Sultan in 1638, when he ordered them to retake Azov from the Don Cossacks. They seem to have felt the same sixty years later. The fall of Azov was indeed a grave blow to the Crimea, but it was an affair of the Turks, and, provided command of Kerch and the sea were main-

---

[1] Khanskaya Ukraine was the name by which the Bessarabians called the rich Ochakov steppe land between the Bug and the Dniester and Yagorlyk; A, A. Kochubinsky, *Osterman i razdyel Turtsii*, app., xxxiv. It was occupied by the Edisan horde of Nogai Tatars.

[2] K. D. Smirnov, *op. cit.*, 650-57, 663-64: Hammer-Purgstall, *Histoire de l'empire ottomane*, xii, 405.

[3] A. A. Novoselsky, "Zemsky sobor 1639 g.", in *Istoricheskie Zapiski*, 1947, xxiv, 18-19; and compare his *Borba moskovskogo gosudartsva s tatarami v pervoi polovinye xvii v.* (Moscow; 1948), 268-71, 288-90.

tained, the overland danger to the Cossacks was greater from the side of the lower Dnieper.

By the treaty of Constantinople (1700) the Tatars were at least relieved of Russian garrisons in the four Turkish forts: but they were lost to the Turks: they were to be razed by the Russians, but not reoccupied by the Turks. Further north, on the left bank, over against the Sech, Kamenny Zaton remained a powerful symbol of the new Russian advance southwards. Recourse was again sought to the ineffective compromise of an unoccupied zone of steppe between the territories of the two countries. Worst of all, the treaty of 1700 contained a clause acknowledging Peter's refusal to recognize the khan's claim to annual tribute. Nothing so infuriated Devlet-Girei and his successors, and the question of tribute proved an irreducible source of conflict for the rest of Peter's reign. His success in 1700 was a turning point in Russian relations with the Crimea. This claim to annual tribute was never admitted again, even after the capitulation on the Pruth.

Peter secured at the same time (1700) an equal success in securing from the Sultan the right to permanent diplomatic representation at Constantinople, on the same footing as the missions of the other powers. This was another novelty and another turning point, and I shall say more of it later. Tolstoi, who was sent to occupy the new post on the Bosphorus, had more than enough on his hands, but he acquitted himself ably. It was a major error of Peter's rival, Charles XII, that he took no steps to secure the same right for Sweden.

The war with Sweden inevitably shifted the main brunt of Peter's energies to the North, and it added considerably to the complexities of putting into force the treaty of Constantinople. He was forced on to the defensive, and his main object was to prevent a resumption of war by the Turks and, if he failed in this, to be in sufficient strength to hold on to his new gains in the South. The Great Northern War did not stop—though it did retard—Peter's projects at Voronezh and Taganrog and Azov.[1] The

---

[1] A glimpse of the burden of labour service at Azov and Taganrog (quite apart from Voronezh) can be seen from the following figures given in a report from Ivan Tolstoi, governor of Azov; text in S. Elagin, *op. cit.*, ii, 343. They also show how very far short the actual numbers at work fell short of what was demanded.

creation of the fleet continued, fortification work was pressed on, and renewed demands were put forward for freedom of navigation in the Black Sea. Here again Peter the Great set a precedent, though it did not come to fulfilment until Catherine the Great.[1]

The Turks were much alarmed by the appearance of a Russian fleet in the Sea of Azov and the portent of the contumacious *Kryepost* in the Golden Horn. The Cossacks in their light "seagull" galleys had often enough in the past proved redoubtable raiders in the Black Sea; now Peter's galleys were added, and the sudden novelty of his war fleet foreshadowed a much more serious threat. The Turks were determined that the Black Sea should be preserved "as a pure and immaculate virgin",[2]

Demanded for labour	*Labourers*	*Skilled artisans*	*Total*
1704	25,500	4,870	30,370
1705	31,262	1,026	32,288
1706	33,146	4,062	37,208
1707	23,416	2,850	26,266
1708 winter	1,500	—	1,500
1709	18,100	—	18,100
Appeared for work			
1704	16,110	586	16,696
1705	16,012	452	16,466
1706	7,082	197	7,279
1707	8,215	170	8,385
1708 winter	1,350	—	1,350
1709	405	—	405
Did not appear for work			
1704	9,390	4,284	13,674
1705	14,466	572	14,822
1706	26,064	3,865	29,929
1707	15,210	2,680	17,882
1708 winter	150	—	150
1709	17,695	—	17,695

There are certain minor discrepancies between the detailed figures and the totals, but these do not alter the general picture. Thus, the percentage of the number demanded who actually came was in 1704 about 55, in 1705 about 50, in 1706 about 20, in 1707 about 30. The drop in 1706 may be due to the effect of the Astrakhan rising. The Bulavin rising, 1707-08, had a catastrophic effect. The report does not state for how long the men were working, but the normal period was April—September, when the men returned home.

[1] Both Voznitsyn and Ukraintsev had demanded freedom of navigation of the Black Sea, unsuccessfully: H. Uebersberger *Russlands Orientpolitik in den letzten zwei Jahrhunderten* (Stuttgart; 1913), 70-73; Bogoslovsky, *op. cit.*, v, 149-53, 215, 157-8.

[2] Ukraintsev report from Constantinople, 18 July, 1700, text in Ustryalov, *op. cit.*, iii, 551. Dositheus reported, 24 Oct., 1699, that the Turks despised Peter's ships of the line in comparison with the Venetian, but feared raids by his galleys; text in Elagin, *op. cit.*, i, 447. The Russians were not the first to demand freedom of navigation in the Black Sea: the British, Dutch and Venetians had done likewise.

and were adamant in rejecting alike Russian demands for freedom of navigation in the Black Sea and for the cession of Kerch. They proceeded to build a new fortress, designed by a Modenese renegade, Galoppo,[1] to command the narrow strait, and had plans even for damming it. On the diplomatic front they countered repeated Russian proposals for free navigation with demands for the razing of Azov and Taganrog and the cessation of shipbuilding at Voronezh.[2] Force, not diplomatic interchanges, was to decide this issue, but it was force of armies not navies. Peter's Azov fleet never fought in action.

This fact, however, does not mean that the fleet was not of much concern to the Turks and the Tatars, and Peter certainly set great store on it as a means of holding them in check and preventing their forces joining with Charles XII. It appears to have been used to much effect in the most critical months before Poltava (February—May, 1709). Peter multiplied orders for the

---

Obviously, however, owing to the geographical position of Russia her demand was on a different footing from any other. At this same time the Aegean caused even more concern to the Turks than the Black Sea owing to the Venetian reconquest of the Morea: "they have an unsleeping eye for the Mediterranean Sea", as Tolstoi reported (1703: Krylova, *loc. cit.*, 255), and the fleet was being strengthened mainly with an eye to depriving the Venetians of their gains. This was in fact achieved in 1714-15.

[1] *e.g.* Hurmazaki, *Documente . . .*, supplement i, 359, report of French minister in Constantinople, 10 May, 1705. Galoppo was to superintend the new fortifications of Bender when Yenikale (Kerch) was finished. Bender was in fact refortified, but I do not know whether by Galoppo.

[2] Krylova, *loc. cit.*, 251, 257, 260. It is shown in the same article, from the evidence of the Russian foreign office archives, that on two occasions Peter was at least prepared to make play with concessions to the Turks as to the fleet. In 1704 during negotiations for a commercial treaty (the first such ever conducted between Russia and Turkey) Peter seems to have been ready to sell part of the Azov fleet if he could get a favourable treaty which would have included a clause as to freedom of navigation in the Black Sea (*loc. cit.*, 265-66). In December 1703, at a moment when the Turks appeared to be very bellicose, Tolstoi was very secretly empowered in the last resort, as a means of warding off war, to offer to remove the fleet from the sea of Azov or to sell it to the Turks, and in addition to offer to raze Kamenny Zaton, but not Taganrog (*loc. cit.*, 267). Even if these concessions were meant seriously, they were only partial: Peter would have kept his ships building at Voronezh and there was no abandonment of his far-reaching plans for the development of Taganrog. In fact much of his existing fleet was of little use. This is probably the clue to Peter's offers of sale. K. D. Smirnov, *op: cit.*, 707-08, states, without giving date, that a Turkish mission was sent from Constantinople to inspect twelve ships offered for sale by Tolstoi. This is probably the same mission as that mentioned as coming in the spring of 1703 to spy out the condition of the Russian fleet, in S. Elagin, *Istoriya russkogo flota*, 196.

strengthening of the fleet, for more than doubling the land forces at Azov, and for preparing for a combined naval and military expedition. He went down south in person from Voronezh to Azov and Taganrog, and in May, two months before Poltava was to be fought, demonstratively displayed his naval preparations before a Turkish envoy. The Sultan replied by forbidding Devlet-Girei to assist Mazepa and the Zaporozhian Cossacks and steered clear of committing himself to Charles XII's alliance schemes.[1]

On the other hand, when it did come to war two years later, the immense efforts that had been lavished on the Azov fleet bore no fruit. There was no subsidiary offensive from Azov, or down the Dnieper. The Tatars were not prevented from appearing in strength on the Pruth. At sea the offensive was taken by the Turks, who were much superior in number and size of ships. Only four Russian ships of the line were in a fit state to put to sea, and they had to be largely manned by soldiers. The Turks reconnoitred Taganrog and besieged Azov. Both put up a stout defence but the Turks were foiled not by Peter's fleet, but by his land forces.[2]

The defeat on the Pruth entailed the loss of the fleet and the cession, not merely the razing, of Azov and Taganrog.[3] Peter never regained them. They were recaptured in 1736, but they

[1] B. Kafenhaus, "Poltavskaya bitva", in *Istorik Marksist*, 1939, iv, 49, citing *Trudy russkago voenno-istoricheskago obshchestva*, iii, *Dokumenty severnoi voiny*, 246-47, 254, 256-57. For Tolstoi's reports at this time on the Turkish attitide; Soloviev, *op. cit.*, xv, 1535-38. Krylova, *loc. cit.*, 269-70, also using the Russian archives, shows that Tolstoi remained cool and collected, discounted the hostile intentions of the Turkish government, and used to good effect the extra large sums with which he was provided for buying off the Turks.

[2] Elagin, *op. cit.*, 235-37. Peter entertained the fantastic hope of pitting against the Turks nineteen ships of the line. Actually only six were able to sail down the Don and join the few small ships available there. Four eighty gun ships were held up owing to low water. Three forty-eight gun ships laid down in 1709 were still uncompleted. The Turks on the other hand appeared off Azov with eighteen men of war and fourteen galleys. *Ibidem*, 231-32, 236-37. There is a description of the siege by the Jesuit Father John Milan, who was in Azov at the time, in a letter to Father John Miller written later when he was in Moscow, 17 August, 1712; *Pisma i Doneseniya Iezuitov o Rossii* . . . (St. Petersburg; 1904), 374-76.

[3] In the end, when after protracted delays, they were handed over to the Turks in the course of 1712, the Russians were successful in making the best of a bad job. They sold to the Turks the stores, guns and powder at Taganrog and they also sold two men of war and two snows, the only ones really worth much, for a high price: Elagin, *op. cit.*, 239 and *prilozheniya*, ii, 142-46.

were left by the treaty of Belgrade (1739) destroyed and unoccupied by either side, and no Russian ships were to be allowed in
the sea of Azov. Not till the triumphs of Catherine the Great's
first Turkish war did Russia once again secure the mouth of the
Don, and at the same time (1774) gain the right to free navigation
of the Black Sea. It is a fantastic irony that it should have been
not Peter's southern fleet, his first-born, still-born, child and
the sucker of such heavy sacrifices, but Peter's Baltic fleet, an
even greater vampire of yet more colossal labours, that fifty years
later fought the first Russian sea action against a Turkish fleet,
not in the Black Sea, but in the Aegean when it won the overwhelming victory of Cnesme (1770). Russia's Black Sea fleet was
the achievement not of Peter, but of Catherine.[1] Once, in his
early days, in 1698, Peter, when at Voronezh, indefatigably
spurring on the building of his fleet despite wholesale desertions
of the labour force and terrible sickness wastage, despite short-
ages of almost every kind and draining costs, despite embittered
hostility, once, but once only, Peter gave vent to despondency:
"Only a cloud of doubt still covers my mind, whether this our
fruit will not bear too late, like dates, which the planters do not
succeed in seeing."[2]

III

RUSSIA AND THE ORTHODOX

IN considering Peter the Great's relations with the Ottoman
Empire I have placed the main emphasis on the problems
arising out of the Crimean Tatars, the Cossacks, Poland, Azov,
and the southern steppes. Some of these problems were new;

---

[1] Although Peter's southern fleet of men of war bore no fruit until the end of
Catherine's reign and the foundation of Sebastopol and Nikolaiev after the incor-
poration of the Crimea (1783), his use of shallow draft flotillas (which was not in
itself a novelty, but the extension of Cossack practice) was followed on a large scale
in the war of 1736-39, both in the sea of Azov against the Crimea and (for the transport of supplies) on the Dnieper and at Ochakov; Manstein, *Memoirs of Russia*
(London; 1773), 123-24, 168, 174-76, 209, 144, 161, 164. So too in both Catherine's
wars against the Turks.
[2] Peter to Vinnius, 14 November, 1698, text in Ustryalov, *op. cit.*, iii, 249.

most were not. I have laid stress in passing on three long-stand-ing counts of Russia against the Crimea, raids, prisoners and annual tribute. These may seem at first sight small matters in comparison with the role of Russia as "the third Rome" who should rescue her Orthodox brothers groaning under the yoke of the Moslem, but they were in actuality both chronologically prior to the dramatic appearance in 1711 of Peter in Moldavia at the head of his would-be liberating army and of far more practi-cal importance for Russia of that day than the wider claims and more far-reaching projects which only later were to become central issues in Russo-Turkish relations. Until Russia was solidly established in the Black Sea and North Causasus steppes, she could not with any real effect play the part urged upon her for the most part only by various Orthodox ecclesiastics in the Balkans and by a handful of Georgians and Armenians in the Caucasus.

This is not, however, to deny either the importance for the future or the lively contemporary apprehension of Russian action as the champion of the Orthodox. Peter the Great made a most notable advance on previous Russian claims and action, even though the disaster on the Pruth destroyed for many decades to come any practical results. Peter's knitting of closer relations with the Balkan Christians was a marked feature of his policy well before 1711. It was one that was much commented upon by contemporaries, and Russian antagonists in Constantinople made regular play with warnings to the Porte against the activi-ties of Tolstoi and Russian agents in priming the Orthodox for eventual revolt in support of Russian arms. Both the range and the effectiveness of the incipient Russian information service and of Russian propaganda were greatly exaggerated, but there was a core of truth in the accusations. The vital success of Peter in 1700 in winning the right to a resident diplomatic mission in Constantinople increased the danger.[1] The fact that in 1711 for

---

[1] Peter's instructions of 12 April, 1702, to Tolstoi, on going to Constantinople, are a revealing example of the range and thoroughness of Peter's desire for informa-tion. It is curious that there is no specific mention of the attitude of the Balkan Christians. The Slavs are not mentioned as such. Apart from political conditions, the main emphasis is on economic conditions, trade with Persia, military and naval organization and plans, the straits of Kerch, European training of cavalry and in-

the first time the Russian tsar marched into the sultan's dominions
to within forty miles of the Danube, took Moldavia momentarily
under his sway, and issued a rousing appeal to the Balkan Christians to rise against the infidel was a great flash of lightning that
disclosed a grim forewarning to the Ottomans of what might roll
up against them in the shape of thunderstorms to come.

Far less dramatic, yet also heavily charged with trouble for the
future, were the first claims that Peter put forward in relation
to the Orthodox, claims for freedom of pilgrimage to the Holy
Land, for Greek possession of the Holy Places, and for a guarantee
of religious freedom for the Orthodox. The first of these claims
was not new; the other two were.

The Russian right to unhindered pilgrimage to the Holy Land
had already been put forward before Peter's day, and equivocal
assent had been given by the Turks in the treaty of Bakhchi-Sarai
(1681).[1] Peter succeeded in procuring definite provision for the
right in the treaty of Constantinople of 1700, though Tolstoi had
considerable difficulty in getting the right translated into practice.
It was lost by the treaty of Adrianople (1713), but Dashkov
regained it in the second treaty of Constantinople (1720), and
thereafter it was not in dispute, save as regards detailed applica-
tion. The matter was not of great import, for Russian pilgrimages to the Holy Land seem to have been rare, if not very rare.[2]

fantry, the fortifications of Ochakov, Akkerman (Belgorod) and Kilia, and any
opposition among "the Sultan's subjects . . . in eastern countries". Text in *Pisma
i Bumagi* . . . , ii, 30—34. No doubt there may have been supplementary instructions
dealing specifically with the Balkan Christians, but, as far as I am aware, none such
have been published.
    [1] "It will be observed according to the ancient custom": text of the articles,
in Italian, as agreed to by the Sultan, in Hammer-Purgstall, *op. cit.*, xii, 502-04.
    [2] There are accounts by four Russian contemporaries of Peter of their pilgrim-
ages to the Holy Land. Ioann Lyukanov, *Puteshestvie v Svyatuyu Zemlyu staroobryadtsa
moskovskago svyashchennika* (Moscow; 1862; also printed in *Russky Arkhiv*, 1863).
He travelled with a "passport" issued by Peter referring to the treaty rights of
Russian pilgrims. Assuming that the dates which he gives are correct, he left
Moscow at a very inauspicious moment, in January 1711, just after Turkey had
declared war, of which he makes no mention. He travelled via the Ukraine and
Moldavia to Tulcha on the Danube, thence by sea to Constantinople, Egypt and
Palestine. He was fourteen weeks in and near Jerusalem. His account of Joppa,
Jerusalem and Bethlehem is detailed and for the most part descriptive, with not
much rhetorical abuse of the Latins or the backsliding Orthodox. He seems to
have been shocked mainly by the mingling of Greeks and "heretics" and their
sharing of churches, and by the installation of an organ in the Church of the Holy

Pilgrimages within Russia were, and continued to be, extremely popular, but the difficulties of the journey to Palestine, which had to be made overland to European Turkey and then by sea, were very great, and the Greeks had no particular reason to encourage pilgrimages from Russia unless they would bring extra money to them. Russia had long been a most valuable source of financial support for Greek ecclesiastics, and notably for the Holy Places, from alms given by the Muscovite government and from the sale

Sepulchre by "the French". He does not refer to demands for the return of the Holy Places to the Greeks. He left Jerusalem on his homeward journey at the end of January 1712, travelling by sea to Damietta and thence by Rhodes to Constantinople, by sea to Kilia, and then overland. In Constantinople, as would be expected of any devout Russian, and all the more so of an Old Believer, he contrasted Greek ways and ritual very unflatteringly with Russian. The patriarchate is very unfavourably described, and he was shocked by the intercourse with papists and by the highest ecclesiastics playing cards and chess.

Vasily Grigorovich-Barsky, *Puteshestvie k Svyatym Myestam* . . . (St. Petersburg; fifth ed., 1800: the first ed. was 1778). He began his journey in 1723 and did not return until 1747, and during this time became a monk in Antioch. He was in Palestine from September 1726 to May 1727, and visited Jerusalem again in 1729. He visited Sinai (the support of which by the Romanovs began in 1687). He was by origin from Kiev and set out with a recommendation from the Archbishop of Lvov, but not from anybody in Russia itself. He travelled from Kiev westwards, through Austria and Italy to the Aegean and the Balkans, including Athos, and went to Jerusalem from Salonika via Cyprus. His book, which runs to eight hundred pages, is a mine of information on churches and monasteries, but (as far as I can judge from a brief perusal) does not throw light on the relations of Russians and the Orthodox in Turkey or on the struggle for the Holy Places. Neither he nor Lyukanov mention meeting other Russian pilgrims.

Matvyei Gavrilovich Nechaev *Khozhdenie vo* . . . *Ierusalim* . . . (Warsaw; 1875). I am much indebted to Mr. F. F. Seeley for the following particulars on Nechaev's record of his pilgrimage. Nechaev was a Yaroslavl burgher, who had taken a vow to make a pilgrimage to Jerusalem and eventually set out in 1721 from Kiev. He went via Jassy and Galatz to Constantinople, and thence in two French ships to Cyprus and Jaffa. He arrived in Jerusalem in March, 1722, and returned by the same route as that by which he had come. Like Lyukanov, he comments with astonishment on the playing of the organ by "the French". He describes which of the Holy Places are in the hands of which confessions, but does not comment directly on the struggle between the Orthodox and the Latins. He does, however, retail an account he was given of Orthodox-Armenian rivalry eighty years earlier. He mentions Greek, Bulgarian and Serbian pilgrims in the Holy Land, but not Russians. Elsewhere on his journey he came across a few Russians, but not pilgrims. In writing of Constantinople, he bursts out into a flight of poetical rhetoric lamenting its fallen glory and hoping for its restoration. His account is full of miscellaneous information, anecdotes and stories, but is not significant for light thrown on religious or political controversies.

I have not been able to find a copy of the fourth account of a pilgrimage to the Holy Land by a contemporary of Peter—Silvestr and Nikodim, *Opisanie puteshestviya* . . . *v Tsargradye i Ierusalim v* 1721 g. (Kiev; 1883: also in *Trudy Kievskoi Dukhovnoi Akademii*, 1883).

of relics.[1] What was wanted for the Holy Places was not so much
pilgrimages as a power to support Greek claims to their custody.
Russia now for the first time appeared as that power.

In 1690, thanks to prolonged efforts on the part of French
diplomacy, the Latins had been accorded the dominant position
in the Holy Places. This reversed what had been the situation
since 1639, when the Greeks after nearly ten years of seesaw
struggle had secured from the sultan the major rights in Jerusalem
and Bethlehem. The earlier predominance of the Latins (in effect
the Franciscans) had been shaken by internecine disputes among
the Catholics owing to the appearance of the Jesuits in Palestine
(1605) and to the activities of the newly created Congregatio de
propaganda fide (1622), and had been challenged by the Greek
ecclesiastical and cultural revival most powerfully personified in
Cyril Lukaris, patriarch of Constantinople. As a result the
Greeks gained the upper hand in 1639. Now in 1690 the fruits
of victory had been lost, and the immediate outcome was an
outpouring from Dositheus, patriarch of Jerusalem, who denounced the French for seizing the Holy Places and behaving
"worse than the Persians and the Arabs".[2] His diatribes had at
least the effect that early in 1692 a Russian envoy in the Crimea

---

[1] Throughout the seventeenth century alms were given on a large scale to
Greeks coming to Russia for them, who supplied in return information (for what
it was worth) on Turkish affairs. Alms, which included keep and transport while
in Russia, were distributed by the *posolsky prikaz* (foreign office). There was no
kind of check on how the alms were really spent. The patriarchs of Constantinople
and Jerusalem and other high dignitaries depended in part for their living upon
such gifts from Russia. An edict of Peter in 1725 attempted to regularize matters
and entrusted all payments to the Holy Synod; these later became known as "Palestine moneys". The purveying of relics to Russia was a brisk and profitable trade.
Various Greek ecclesiastics (most notably Paisius Ligarides) made a temporary
living in Russia under false pretences. Peter issued a number of edicts designed
to control more strictly the entry of Greeks and to prevent pretenders. Probably
he suspected Turkish use of Greeks as spies. Nepluyev in 1723 reported that the
Turks had sent in Greeks ostensibly to beg alms who really were spies, and in 1712
two Greek traders were said to have been sent in by them at Swedish instigation
to murder Peter. There is an earlier case in 1671 known of a Greek trader being
accused of being a Turkish janissary spy in disguise. N. Th. Kapterev, *Kharakhter
otnoshenii Russii k pravoslavnomu vostoku XVI i XVII stolyetikakh* (Sergiev Posad;
2nd ed., 1914), 145, 221-47, 271-75, 346-48. Cited hereafter as *Kharakhter* . . . .

[2] Report of Dositheus to Moscow, 29 March, 1691, received in September;
extract in Soloviev, *op. cit.*, xv, 1143-45, also summarized in Kapterev, *Snosheniya*
. . . , 281-84. His first report on the Holy Places, sent in November 1690, received
28 April 1691, is summarized pp. 275-81.

included in his peace conditions the return of the Holy Places to the Greeks,[1] the first appearance of a demand from Russia that was later to have such an eventful history.

The demand of 1692, as far as the Muscovite government was concerned, was almost solely for form's sake, and Dositheus's continued bombardment had little result.[2] The same demand was indeed repeated in instructions to Voznitsyn and Ukraintsev, but it was not pressed, and Ukraintsev accepted without over much difficulty vague assurances as to the future.[3] It was kept on the list of Russian claims, for it might come in useful as a bargaining counter; and so it did in 1709 when Tolstoi tided over an awkward outburst of the Turks by withdrawing a request recently made by Peter for the handing over of the keys of the Holy Sepulchre to the Greeks.[4] Thereafter the demand slumbered in the files. Dositheus was dead; Russian relations with the Greek hierarchy became strained and insignificant; the defeat on the Pruth reduced Russia to an uphill defensive, and even after the revival of her position at Constantinople in 1720 Peter did not renew his protests on the Holy Places, a matter in which he displayed no personal interest. None the less his reign marks the beginning of what was to be of much consequence for the future and to fester into one of the broils out of which arose the Crimean War.[5]

[1] Soloviev, *op. cit.*, xiv, 1111-12.
[2] Kapterev, *Snosheniya* . . . , 287-99, 326-30.
[3] Bogoslovsky, *op. cit.*, v, 57, 78, 154, 159, 284.
[4] Hammer-Purgstall, *op. cit.*, xiii, 215; Kapterev, *Snosheniya* . . . , 394-98.
On the Holy Places in the seventeenth and early eighteenth centuries: F. v. Verdy du Vernois, *Die Frage der Heiligen Stätten* (Berlin; 1901), 29-55, succinct and mainly juridical, with excellent map of the Church of the Holy Sepulchre; C. Famin, *Histoire de la rivalité et du protectorat des églises chrétiennes en Orient* (Paris; 1853), 188-264, an unreliable and biassed *oeuvre de circonstance*, but with useful points; Kapterev, *Snosheniya* . . . , 63-86, 111-13 (on the Latin-Greek struggle during the sixteen-thirties); Jorga, *op. cit.*, iv, 17-31 (on 1600—1640); H. Uebersberger, *op. cit.*, 40-42. Most of the firmans, berats, etc., are in Testa, *Recueil des traités de la Porte ottomane*, iii, 313-20. Under Louis XIV support of the Catholics in Palestine and elsewhere in the Ottoman empire was one of the major tasks of the French ministers in Constantinople. The difficulties were very great, and the Latins did not obtain full satisfaction for the carrying out of the firman of 1690 until 1718 when the French minister de Bonnac gained permission for the reconstruction of the Church of the Holy Sepulchre, C. Scheffer, *Mémoire sur l'ambassade de France à Constantinople* . . . (Paris; 1894), xxxix, xlii. De Bonnac emphasized strongly the

Of still more consequence in the future was the third Orthodox claim put forward by Peter, that for a general guarantee of freedom of worship and religion for the Orthodox and of freedom from excessive taxation. It appears for the first time in Russian history in the Karlowitz negotiations and was repeated by Ukraintsev in 1700. The draft article followed very closely a similar draft in regard to the Catholics put forward by the Austrians; but, whereas an amended form of the Austrian article duly figured in the treaty signed by them and the Turks at Karlowitz, the Russians were unable to secure anything corresponding when they concluded their peace eighteen months later in Constantinople.[1] Seventy-four years were to elapse before Catherine the Great succeeded where Peter the Great had failed and wrote into the treaty of Kuchuk-Kainardji a somewhat similar article, which was later to figure so prominently in the origins of the Crimean War.

It was in fact the Orthodox in Poland, not in Turkey, who were the first to feel the protecting hand of Russia. An undertaking against any form of religious oppression of the Orthodox had been given by Poland in the treaty of 1686 with Russia.[2] Already in the early sixteen-nineties petitions began to flow in to Moscow asserting that the article was being contravened. No action was then taken by Moscow, but the situation was very different in the later years of Peter (1718-25) when he was in the ascendancy. New appeals from the Orthodox in Poland were multiplied, and Peter's commissaries were extremely active on their behalf. At

---

obstacles he had to overcome owing to "la jalousie et les artifices des Grecs, la superstition et l'avarice des Turcs, et si je l'ose dire, la politique des Réligieux mêmes de Terre Sainte": *ib.*, 140.

[1] Text of Voznitsyn's draft article in Hurmuzaki, *Fragmente* . . . , iii, 413-15, cf. Bogoslovsky, *op. cit.*, iii, 393-94. It covered the Orthodox in general, but more especially "the Greeks, Serbs, Bulgars, Sclavonians . . . (*Slovakim*)." The Austrian draft article (text, in Latin, in Hurmuzaki, *Documente* . . . , v, pt. 2, 317) specified more detailed provisions in favour of the Catholic religion than those in the treaty of Karlowitz as finally signed (text in Noradounghian, *op. cit.*, i, 189), but, unlike the treaty, it did not include any mention of the extremely important right of representation by the Emperor on behalf of the Catholics. The Russian draft, being modelled on the Austrian draft, likewise did not claim this right. For Ukraintsev's negotiations on this question; Bogoslovsky, *op. cit.*, v, 80, 154-55, 159.

[2] Fifteen years earlier, in 1671, a project for a Russian guarantee had been sent to Moscow from the Ukraine, together with appeals against Catholic oppression; V. Einhorn, *Ocherki iz istorii Malorossii v xvii v.* (Moscow; 1899), i, 772-78.

the close of his life, in 1724, the "massacre" at Thorn was given international importance, largely owing to Russian action. The problem of the Dissidents, so fatal to Poland, was ripening faster than that of the Christians in European Turkey.[1]

IV

RUSSIA, AUSTRIA AND THE BALKAN CHRISTIANS

NONE the less the problem of the Balkan Christians was very much in evidence as a consequence of the great Austrian advances against the Turks between 1683 and 1698. Peter inherited from the regency of his half-sister Sofia a growing volume of appeals from the Orthodox Christians, not only from Greek ecclesiastics (Dositheus at their head) and from varied sources in the Principalities, but from the Serbs.[2] During the Austrian campaigns the Serbs had been roused to revolt against the Turks and some hundred thousand migrated into southern Hungary. After a swaying struggle, when the Austrian troops were finally withdrawn north of the Danube, these Serbs found their hopes of return to their homelands dashed by the treaty of Karlowitz. The Serbian church and its patriarchate of Peć (Ipek), which were the centre of Serbian national feelings, were in effect divided.[3] and the Serbs in Hungary had to make the best they could of the emperor Leopold's diplomas granting them privileges,

---

[1] Soloviev, op. cit., xiv, 986 (1686), 1128-32 (1690-94), xvii, 536-37, 547-49, xviii, 706-16 (1718—1724); *Cambridge History of Poland, 1797—1935* (Cambridge; 1941), 17—19.

[2] Earlier in the seventeenth century connections with the Serbs had been almost entirely confined to fairly frequent and fairly sucessful visits to Muscovy of Serbian ecclesiastics in search of financial support; L. Hadrovics, *Le peuple serbe et son église sous la domination turque* (Paris; 1947), 103-105, 114-16, 127-28.

[3] After the flight to the Austrians in 1690 of Arsenius III Crnojević, patriarch of Peć, the Turks secured the nomination of a successor, a Greek by origin, and the patriarchate continued at Peć until 1766, when it was suppressed and the Serbian church in the Ottoman dominions was placed under the jurisdiction of the patriarch of Constantinople. The position of the patriarchs of Peć was extremely weak, while that of Arsenius and his successors, as supreme metropolitans of Karlovci (Karlowitz) in southern Hungary, was very considerably stronger. Hadrovics, *op. cit.*, 147-54.

diplomas based on the Turkish berats to the Serbian church.[1] Despite these privileges, they suffered from Austrian attempts to turn them from the Orthodox to the Catholic faith. Hedged in between the Austrians and the Turks they might perhaps gain something from the Russians, even if it were only financial help, an important end in itself.

The most striking feature of the appeals to Russia from the Balkan Orthodox is that they were directed quite as much against Catholic Austria as against Moslem Turkey—which did not seek proselytes. The metropolitan of Skoplje, who made his way to Moscow in 1687, inveighed against the dangers of Austrian domination and the ill-treatment of refugee Serbian bishops in Hungary. He was followed next year by Isaiah, archimandrite of St. Paul's monastery on Athos, imploring Russia to save the Orthodox from Latin as well as Moslem conquerors, and bringing appeals for help not only from Constantinople and Sherban Cantacuzene, hospodar of Wallachia, but as well from Arsenius Crnojević, the Serbian patriarch of Peć (Ipek).[2] The further successes of the Empire against the Turks added to Orthodox alarms. "We all pray with tears" ran one letter in 1698, "for the sovereign monarch to save us from the Papists and Jesuits, who rage against the Orthodox more than against the Turks and Jews. . . . The secular war may finish some time, but the Jesuit war never."[3] Prince Eugène's overwhelming victory on the Zenta stimulated yet more fears that liberation would come from "the Swabians", which would mean no liberation.

The hopes of easy success and of a rising of the Christians in support of Orthodox Russia were dangled before the eyes of

[1] Hadrovics, op. cit., 144.

[2] Uebersberger, op. cit., 42-48; Kapterev, Kharakhter . . . , 369-79; Soloviev, op. cit., xiv, 1017-18. Peter himself came into contact with Patriarch Arsenius during his visit to Vienna in 1698. Arsenius asked for pressure on the Emperor to keep his promises to the Serbs, and supplied Voznitsyn with an intermediary with the Turks at the Karlowitz negotiations. Peter was also approached by the Serbian "despot" Branković for release from the imprisonment he had been suffering from the Austrians since 1689. Bogoslovsky, op. cit., ii, 507-10; Uebersberger, op. cit., 59-60.

[3] Letter of George Kastriot (envoy of hospodar of Wallachia to Moscow) to Mazepa, enclosed in the letter of Mazepa to L. K. Naryshkin, 17 January, 1698 (received by Peter in Amsterdam, 27 Feb., 1698), extract in Ustryalov, op. cit., iii, 471-72.

Peter as previously before those of Sofia and Golitsyn. Let Sofia play the part of Deborah, Judith and Esther.[1] Let Peter follow the example of Gideon and his three hundred against the hosts of Midian.[2] The Russians were not unwary enough to be carried away as yet into playing any such roles. Sofia and Golitsyn had not attempted more than the Crimea, which proved far beyond their strength, and in 1689 their undoing. Peter struck for Azov, at the furthest remove from the Balkan lands. His further plans were ruined by the determination of his ally Austria to have her hands free for action in the West. She signed peace with the Turks at Karlowitz, and Poland and Venice followed suit. As has been already emphasized, Peter was infuriated at what he regarded as the treachery of his ally. Thus the first Austro-Russian alliance—which was an alliance for *offensive* action against Turkey—foundered almost before the ink was dry. The rivalry of the two countries in the Balkans dates from Peter's time; but it was not solely an external rivalry injected into the Balkans; as has just been suggested, it had roots among the Balkan peoples themselves and was plentifully nourished by them.

Mutual hostility, or at best suspicion, continued throughout Peter's reign. His intrigues with Rákóczy and the Hungarians inspired the worst feelings in Vienna. On occasion the Russian diplomats took up the idea of urging Turkey to renew war with Austria, as a useful lightning conductor.[3] After the Turks finally did so in 1716 (not with Russian prompting), Dashkov made great play at Constantinople with the assertion that his master had resolutely refused overtures from Vienna to ally himself with Austria and Venice.[4] The rift was widened by the

---

[1] Letter of Dionysius, ex-patriarch of Constantinople, to Sofia, 1688, extract in Kapterev, *Kharakhter* . . . , 370.

[2] Letter of Dositheus, patriarch of Jerusalem, to Peter, 1698, *ib.*, 510.

[3] Golovin, Peter's foreign minister, suggested this to Tolstoi at the end of 1703, but Tolstoi did not act on it. At the end of 1706 Tolstoi himself renewed the suggestion, in conjunction with the French, but nothing came of it. French policy changed in 1707 and was henceforward directed towards stirring up Turkey against Russia. Krylova, *loc. cit.*, 263, 268, from the Russian archives.

[4] Dashkov, 1719: *ib.*, 278; Zinkeisen, *Geschichte des osmanischen Reiches in Europa*, v, 583, 587-88; Hurmuzaki, *Documente* . . . , vi, 288, text, in Latin, of Dashkov's memorandum given to grand vizier at his first audience. Cf. in regard to Venice in 1716, Hurmuzaki, *Fragmente* . . . , iv, 92.

Mecklenburg dispute, by the flight of the tsarevich Alexis to Austria and the resultant embroilments, by mutual jealousies as to Poland, and by Charles VI's sharing in George I's combination against Russia. Only at the very end of Peter's reign did a change begin to set in. Affairs in the Caucasus were not going well. France ceased her support at Constantinople. Turkey seemed all too likely to fight. As a result the Austrian party in St. Petersburg gained ground, and a year after Peter's death Osterman succeeded in making the second alliance with Austria. It was to last for thirty-five years, through one war with Turkey (1735-39), and through the Seven Years' War, but, as the treaty of Belgrade (1739) showed only too painfully for Russia, the counteracting pull of imperial interests in the West and mutual rivalry in the Balkans, especially the Principalities, were just as prominent as in Peter's day.

At that time, in the sixteen-nineties, Peter had not responded to the high-flown summonses to bold action that reached him through the Principalities or the Serbs. Attack Ochahov, "the key of the Black Sea, more necessary than Azov," they urged. Invade the Budzhak, hold the Perekop isthmus, but do not attempt a conquest of the Crimea itself: join up with the Moldavians and Wallachians, who will rise and hold the line of the Danube: 300,000 Bulgars and Serbs will join in arms against the Moslems—and against "the Germans".[1] These were but specious hopes, but it was true that, with Austrian troops on the Danube, Russia could not play the major role with the Balkan Christians while her troops were hundreds of miles away on the Dnieper and the Don. Peter did indeed order some reconnoitring of the Black Sea coast from the Dnieper estuary to the mouths of the Danube. A year later, when Ukraintsev was sent to Constantinople (1699), he was ordered, if peace proved impossible, to consult with Dositheus as to continuing the war and marching to Kilia on the Danube with the assistance of the Christians.[2]

---

[1] Ustryalov, *op. cit.*, iii, 477-78: Uebersberger, *op. cit.*, 43.
[2] Ustryalov, *op. cit.*, iii, 478, 281.

V

THE PRINCIPALITIES AND THE PRUTH CAMPAIGN

PEACE did not prove impossible in 1700, but when it did in 1711 this was precisely what Peter attempted to do. The war of 1711 was not of Peter's seeking. Two years before, when he had won the battle of Poltava, "a very outstanding and unexpected victory", in which "the whole army of Phaetons received their quittance",[1] Charles XII took refuge in Ottoman territory at Bender. Mazepa, accompanying him, died early in the autumn of 1709, but the remnant of his Cossacks elected in his stead as ataman Philip Orlik, who resolutely devoted the rest of his life to playing the role of an Ukrainian Rákóczy.[2] The Zaporozhian Cossacks, who had joined Mazepa and Charles before Poltava and had suffered in retaliation by Peter the complete destruction of the Sech, had sought Turkish protection in the Kinburn peninsula.[3] Devlet Girei was still khan of the Crimea, and still as ever bent on war with Russia. Thus the steppe lands of the Ottoman empire were enflamed. "The King of Sweden has fallen like a heavy weight upon the shoulders of the Sublime Porte". So runs a Turkish document.[4] But it took Charles a year and more to drive the Sultan to war.

In Constantinople Poltava made a great impression, though it

---

[1] Autograph letter of Peter to F. M. Apraxin, 8 July, 1709, text in Golikov, *Dyeyaniya Petra Velikago*, xv, 396-98. He repeats these expressions in several other letters written at the same time.

[2] For Orlik, and particularly his relations with England, see E. Borshak, "Early Relations between England and Ukraine", in *Slavonic Review*, 1931, x, 149-57.

[3] "I have ordered . . . also that all their abodes be destroyed, so that this nest of traitors be utterly uprooted"; report of Menshikov, quoted in Soloviev, *op. cit.* xv, 1546: *cf.* W. E. D. Allen, *The Ukraine* (Cambridge; 1940), 196-97, 208-09. D. Doroshenko, *History of the Ukraine* (Edmonton; 1939), 396, emphasises the importance of the fact that, before Poltava, Peter succeeded in destroying the Zaporozhian river flotilla at Perevolochnaya, with the result that the Swedes after defeat at Poltava were unable to cross the Dnieper in any numbers and capitulated at Perevolochnaya.

[4] Hammer-Purgstall, *op. cit.*, xiii, 217.

also caused much alarm. Tolstoi won the first round and secured the renewal of the 1700 treaty, with the addition of a clause stipulating the return of Charles to Sweden. But thereafter the internal struggle among the Turks turned against the Russians. Charles had acquired money;[1] he had the active support of the French; and he had two able envoys in Constantinople, Poniatowski, an adherent of Lesczyński, Charles's puppet king of Poland, and Neugebauer, a German propagandist adventurer, who after a spell of service with Peter had left Russia with embittered hostility. Poniatowski gained the ear of Fonseca, the Portuguese Jewish doctor of the sultan, and enlisted the aid of the aged Sultana Valide, urging on her son the sultan to help "her lion", as she styled Charles, devour the tsar.[2] The increasingly close relations of Peter with the Principalities added to Turkish fears. In July, 1710, the pacific grand vizier Ali Pasha lost his post. In the autumn "the northerners", headed by Devlet-Girei, finally won the day, and Achmet declared war in November.[3]

Peter had been pressing him hard for the departure of Charles, and finally did indeed use the threat of war, but the messenger never reached Constantinople, and Peter, whatever his ultimate designs against Turkey, had no desire whatever to plunge into war in the South at this juncture when so much still remained to be done in the North against Sweden, even despite his conquest of Viborg, Riga and the Baltic provinces. The appeal that he

[1] On the death of Mazepa, his nephew Voinarovsky handed over to Charles his treasure chest as a loan. Charles also succeeded in securing some money from Holstein and in Constantinople, from the brothers Cook, agents of the Levant Company; Soloviev, *op. cit.*, xvi, 43, 89.

[2] Hammer-Purgstall, *op. cit.*, xiii, 212. She retained her admiration for "her lion" and was in communication with him in March and April 1713; text of two letters from her to Charles, from the Paris archives, in A. N. Kurat, *Izveç Kirali XII Karl' in Turkiyede kaldiği zamana ait metinler ve vesikalar* (Istanbul; 1943), pt. i, 196-98. The first half of this collection of documents is in Turkish, which I am unable to read. For the same reason I have not been able to use Professor Kurat's *Izveç Kirali XII Karl' in Turkiyede kalişi ve bu Siralarda osmanli imparatorluğu* (Istanbul; 1943).

[3] "The great turn in affairs is wholly the work of the *Tartar khan*" (underlined in the original); desp. of Sutton, 20 November (O.S.), 1710, in *P.R.O.*, *S.P.* 97/22. The khan was in Constantinople at the time. It is probable that the decisive factor lay in the struggle for power among the Turks themselves, not in the foreign missions in Constantinople. Much light will undoubtedly be thrown on this period in the forthcoming publication of the despatches of Sutton, the British minister at Constantinople, in the Camden series by Professor A. N. Kurat of Ankara.

now issued to the Balkan Christians to rise was a means to win him support, not an end in itself or part of a carefully timed offensive against the Ottoman empire. He did not react implacably to the Turkish declaration of war, nor to a Crimean raid in force (January, 1711) aiming, unsuccessfully, at the Voronezh shipyards. Inevitably he pushed on hasty preparations for war in the South, but possibilities of mediation were explored, through Great Britain and even Austria, and through France, with whom negotiations continued as late as June,[1] even after formal announcement of war had been solemnly proclaimed in Moscow. This did not take place until 11 March, when the guards paraded with their standards inscribed with the sign of the cross and the inscription "Under this sign we conquer".[2]

The guards did not conquer, but they fought—and fought stoutly—where no Russians had penetrated since the days of Svyatoslav. For the first time for more than seven centuries a Russian army entered Moldavia and Russian cavalry watered their horses in the Danube, when Rönne's corps burnt the grand vizier's magazines at Braila. A generation earlier, in the Chigirin campaigns (1677-78), a Russian army had fought the Turks on the right bank of the Dnieper only about a hundred miles from Kiev, which itself was in danger. Now, in 1711, the Russians were in Jassy, and though they met disaster on the Pruth it was far down the river, well within the Ottoman dominions, five hundred miles from Kiev.[3]

---

[1] Golikov, *op. cit.*, xii, 248-51, text of declaration of Peter to Sultan, 17 January, 1711, pacific in character despite Peter's news of Turkish declaration of war and imprisonment of Tolstoi; *Arkhiv Kurakina*, ii, 36-8, text of declaration of Peter, 11 March, 1711, very moderate in tone, prepared to accept the good offices or mediation of Great Britain and Austria; M. Vassileff, *Russland und Frankreich von der Thronbesteigung Peter des Grossen bis . . . 1717* (Gotha; 1902), 44-52. The French, whether deliberately or through conflicting views, were pursuing a policy of great intricacy, if not duplicity. Desalleurs, the new French minister at Constantinople, arriving from Hungary and closely connected with Rákóczy, had been egging the Turks on to war with Russia. The Russians knew this. Yet Baluze was sent to Russia in the winter of 1710-11 to attempt to secure support for Rákóczy and to secure a peace between Russia, Turkey and Sweden. Peter refused to listen to plans to aid Rákóczy, and was extremely suspicious of the other French design, but he did in the end negotiate with the French, who insisted, however, in including Sweden in mediation, whereas Peter would accept terms with Turkey only.

[2] Soloviev, *op. cit.*, xvi, 57.

[3] The Russians, who were in alliance with Augustus II, entered Moldavia

Peter himself, accompanied by his wife Catherine, was at the head of his army.   He avowed that he had never been "in such desperation" as when surrounded at the battle of Stanelishte, 19-21 July.[1]   This "deadly banquet" cost him dear,[2] though not so dear as he had feared.   In the last resort he would have accepted any terms "except slavery",[3] would have ceded not only Azov to the Turks, but all his conquests from Sweden (in addition Pskov and more), all except Ingria, his "darling paradise" St. Petersburg.[4] The actual terms he had to sign were far less severe, but they were humiliating enough: he lost Azov, Taganrog, his Dnieper forts, his fleet, all that he had gained in 1700.   He was not to intervene in Poland: Charles XII was to have free passage to Sweden. Peter's southern projects were ruined past repair.   "The Lord God drove me out of this place, like Adam out of paradise".[5]

It is doubtful whether bribery on the grand scale, including Catherine's jewels, was mainly responsible for the grand vizier not insisting on much harsher terms.   Baltadji and others were certainly gifted, but that was invariable custom and more investigation is needed as to whether the scale was exceptional. Baltadji certainly lost the viziership a few months later, hotly assailed with charges of rumbling carts loaded with gold for which he sacrificed the interests of the Padishah.[6]   But the charge

---

through the Polish Ukraine, which was only too well known to them and easy going; thereby they avoided the longer and uncertain passage of the nominally Turkish no man's land between the lower Dnieper, the Bug, and the Dniester.   It was across this difficult country that Münich marched in 1738, the next time that the Russians attempted the invasion of Moldavia.   He failed completely, partly from ignorance of where to cross the Dniester.   In the following year, he succeeded brilliantly: then he came through the Polish Ukraine.

[1] Letters of Peter to F. M. Apraxin and to the Senate, 26 July, 1711, text in Golikov, *op. cit.*, xii, 361, 363.

[2] *Ibidem.*

[3] Autograph letter of Peter to Shafirov, in the Turkish camp, 22 July, 1711, text in Golikov, *op. cit.*, xii, 355.

[4] Instructions of Peter to Shafirov, text in Soloviev, *op. cit.*, xvi, 71.

[5] So Peter used to speak of the loss of the Azov-Taganrog region, according to Münich's diary, text in E. Herrmann, *Beiträge zur Geschichte des russischen Reiches* (Leipzig; 1843), 125.

[6] Jorga, *op. cit.*, iv. 311, mentions bribery only in a footnote.   Hammer-Purgstall, *op. cit.*, xiii, 237-38, 243-45, belittles it except as a subsequent Turkish charge against Baltadji.   Uebersberger, *op. cit.*, 109-11, is reserved.   Soloviev, *op. cit.*, xvi, 71, gives without comment the sums authorised to be offered to the grand vizier and others.   It is noteworthy that Poniatowski, the envoy of

seems to have swollen greatly with the lapse of time. The janissaries had had tough fighting and had suffered severely: Rönne's cavalry had raided Braila in the rear of the Turks and burnt their magazines. The bellicose extremism of Devlet-Girei, the Crimean khan, was probably not to the taste of Baltadji, and he must have been doubly anxious to conclude matters with the Russians before the obdurate Charles XII rode in from Bender breathing fire and slaughter. How lamentable it would have been for the already harassed Turks to have had two crowned heads on their hands, had Peter's own fears of captivity been realised ! Baltadji had in fact secured decisive gains for his own master, though not for Devlet or for Charles.

If the reasons for the terms are somewhat doubtful, the reasons for Peter's catastrophe are clear. His information was defective and over-optimistic. His supplies failed completely and he was caught in a drought-stricken stretch of country. The Turks moved more rapidly than expected, and they were far superior in numbers and artillery. They easily won the race for the passage of the Danube. Peter has been accused of rash impetuosity in pushing on south even after he had the news that the Turks had crossed, and he might perhaps have escaped disaster if he had

Lesczinsky and the confidant of Charles XII, who was with the grand vizier at the time, makes no mention of bribery either in his hurried, short letter of 22 July (the treaty was signed the next day) or in his long letter (the beginning of it is apparently missing) of 27 July to Funck, Swedish envoy in Constantinople; texts printed by A. N. Kurat in *Slavonic Review*, 1947, xxvi, 245-48. Likewise, there is even no specific accusation of bribery in Charles XII's letter to the Sultan of 7 August protesting against the peace treaty; nor is there in the reports of Fleischman and Talmann to Vienna of 29 July and 21 August. Fleischman, who did not join the grand vizier until 5 August, does however emphasize bribery in his report to Vienna of 14 September, and so does Talmann in his report of 19 September, stating that the Turks had demanded a large war indemnity but desisted when the Russians made over to the grand vizier "unter der Handt" a large sum of gold. According to Fleischman's report, the Crimean khan only received half what the grand vizier did. Texts of these Austrian reports in Hurmuzaki, *Documente . . .*, vi. 82, 84-6, 94-7, 107-14, 114-23.

Sutton, the British minister, who was in Constantinople, reported on 10 August (O.S.) that, despite the efforts of the Swedes and the remonstrances of Devlet-Girei, the Turks "seem universally well-pleased with the peace in the manner it was concluded". The grand vizier was incensed against Charles XII and almost openly insulting. Sutton's first mention of bribery occurs in his despatch of 4 September (O.S.): "a few of the vulgar only amuse themselves with the reports" of bribery spread by the Swedes and Tatars. His despatch of 21 November (O.S.) records the success of the campaign against the grand vizier. P.R.O., S.P. 97/22.

then beat a retreat.   He did not do so "pour ne pas mettre en désespoir les Chrétiens qui imploraient le secours de sa Majesté".[1] So ran the official version, and it is probably in substance true. Peter miscalculated both the strength of the Turks and above all the effective aid he would receive from the hospodars and from the other Balkan Christians. The vital difficulty lay in this. The Christians might rise and lend effective aid only if the Russians first proved by a defeat of the Turks that they might be on the winning side: but the Russians were not in sufficient force to achieve a victory without substantial help from the Christians.

During the third quarter of the seventeenth century Muscovite relations with Wallachia and especially with Moldavia had been increasingly close, and Peter's father Alexis had received various offers of alliance and even of acceptance of his suzerainty (1654-56, 1674).[2] Muscovy, however, was too involved in the Polish-Ukrainian struggle to stretch out effectively so far to the south-west, and thereafter, apart from cultural links, it was the ascendancy of Austria, not of Muscovy, which bulked largest for the Principalities. By the time of the Great Northern War they were turning towards Peter, but the rivalry between the two hospodars and the divisions among the boyars of Wallachia and to a lesser extent of Moldavia were fatal to any whole-hearted and energetic support of the Russians.

Moldavia, under a succession of rapidly changing rulers, was weaker and poorer than Wallachia, where Brancovan had maintained himself as hospodar ever since 1689. Possessed of great wealth and great diplomatic skill, as well as of a size-able army, he was the prince of trimmers—in the circumstances almost the highest compliment that could be paid to any hos-podar—, although in the end he lost all and was publicly beheaded in Constantinople (1714). Already before Poltava he had begun to trim his sails towards Russia. Shortly after he moved much nearer, and may even perhaps have concluded a close alliance with Peter in the event of war with Turkey. In any case, however,

---

[1] *Journal de Pierre le Grand* . . . , (Berlin; 1773), 369.
[2] A. D. Xénopol, *Histoire des roumains* . . . (Paris; 1896), ii, 71-76, 98-102; I. Cheban, "O vsaimo-otnosheniyakh Moldavii s moskovskom gosudarstvye v xv—xviii vv.", in *Voprosy istorii*, 1945, ii, 62-65.

he was not the man to burn his boats, and he needed ample alternative craft.

His worst enemies were the Cantemirs, a Moldavian boyar family, and Alexander Mavrocordato, for over thirty years the first dragoman of the Porte and one of the leading politicians in Constantinople. In November 1709 there was a change in Moldavia. Michael Rakovitza, the hospodar, was accused of being hand in glove with the Russians and was removed. Nicholas Mavrocordato, the son of Alexander, was selected in his stead, the first of the Phanariot hospodars. This appointment was a direct blow against Brancovan. By the end of 1710, when the Turks had declared war, Nicholas was thought not strong enough, and he was replaced by Demetrius Cantemir, whose task was to remove Brancovan and whose reward would be the much richer Wallachia. Devlet-Girei was heart and soul in this intrigue, denouncing Brancovan before the sultan for his connections with Peter and declaring that he must now be made away with before he and his army went over to the Russians. Cantemir, however, received no explicit orders to act against Brancovan and feared that his rival had, as usual, reinsured himself in Constantinople. This was in fact the case, though Brancovan also tried to reinsure himself with Peter. Attempts by Russian sympathisers to bring the two together failed.

Cantemir himself was persuaded that the star of the Ottomans was declining and that Russia was the rising power. In the utmost secrecy he negotiated with Peter. Cantemir's boyars were divided, but many, probably most, favoured linking up with the Russians. By now they were near at hand, and at last, though not until late in April 1711, Cantemir, instead of acting against Brancovan, acted with Peter and signed two treaties with him. The first provided for alliance and aid in the war and for Moldavia to receive an autonomous status under the military protection of Russia. The second proved to be the more important: it ensured to Cantemir a safe refuge in Russia in case of necessity.

In Wallachia Brancovan was faced with the long standing hostility of Thomas Cantacuzene, who was an adherent of Peter and was anxious, with one section of the boyars, to commit

Wallachia without further waiting on events. Cantacuzene was sent to Peter to denounce Brancovan as a dilatory turncoat and to prepare for Wallachia siding with the Russians. Others, and probably most, of the Wallachian boyars, however, thought differently. As one of them said: "It is dangerous to declare for Russia until the tsar's army crosses the Danube. Who knows, moreover, whether Wallachia in the power of the Russians will be happier than under the domination of the Turks ?"[1] After the battle on the Pruth, one of Brancovan's close adherents wrote in praise of his wisdom in "awaiting the decision of a battle in which it has finally been seen that beneath German clothes the Muscovites are still Muscovites".[2] Here in two nutshells is summed up the reason for Peter's failure to win Wallachia.

The essentials of the situation in the Principalities may be summed up thus. All depended upon the hospodars, the boyars and their leading retainers; unless a clear lead came from these, no appeals for a rising against the Ottoman overlord could incite the main mass of the people. Moldavia, the nearer to Russia but the weaker, under a new hospodar at daggers drawn with the hospodar of Wallachia, proved almost a broken reed as to substantial, organized aid. Wallachia, with large supplies available, badly needed by the Russians, was divided as to the least dangerous course to pursue. Brancovan, under strong suspicion by the Turks and with a healthy respect for the strength of their army in the field, deferred decisive action until as late as possible. Then, when the Turks were across the Danube, he thought best to save himself and his country by truckling to their demands and handing over to them the supplies that had been amassed for the Russians with money furnished by Peter.[3]

---

[1] A. Kochubinsky, *Snosheniya Rossii pri Petrye pervom s yuzhnymi slavyanam i rumunami* (Moscow; 1867), 59; also in *Chteniya moskovskago obshchestva istorii i drevnosti*, 1872, ii.

[2] Hurmuzaki, *Documente . . . .*, supplement i, 414.

[3] The above analysis of the situation in the Principalities is based principally on, Kochubinsky, *op. cit.*, 18-25, 40-75; Uebersberger, *op. cit.*, 91-112; Soloviev *op. cit.*, xvi, 58—74; Xénopol, *op. cit.*, ii, 124-54; and R. W. Seton-Watson, *A History of the Rumanians* (Cambridge; 1934), 70-100.

VI

THE SERBS AND THE MONTENEGRINS.

IF the Rumanian aristocracy, rent with mutual dissensions, did not for the most part risk giving a determined lead to a revolt against their Turkish masters, in the western Balkans there was plenty of *haiduk* material which could easily be set alight, at least with a quick flame if not, save in Montenegro, with a steady core of fire. Among the Serbs and Montenegrins fighting leaders were available, some of whom had been to Russia as agents of revolt and all of whom were accustomed to long odds and desperate ventures. It was among this hardy peasantry alone that Peter's inflammatory appeal to revolt bore fruit.

Between 1704 and 1710 at least four Serbian fighting leaders had made their way to Moscow to knit connections, beg funds, and in at least one case to offer the services of the Serbs "on behalf of their Orthodox tsar ... For in faith and tongue we have no other tsar than God in heaven and on earth the most orthodox tsar Peter."[1] These were a very different type of informant and supporter from the Greek ecclesiastical functionaries and Rumanian princelings and their retainers, on whom the Russians hitherto had largely relied.[2] So too was the man who was at this time Peter's main main adviser and agent for Balkan affairs, Sava Vladislavić, usually known as Raguzinsky. Born in 1668 at Popovo in Herzegovina, he had been brought up in Ragusa in his

---

[1] Soloviev, *op. cit.*, xvi, 61; Hadrovics, *Le peuple serbe et son église sous la domination turque*, 125; S. Bogoyavlensky, "Iz russko-serbskikh otnoshenii pri Petrye pervom", in *Voprosy istorii*, 1946, viii-ix, 25; Uebersberger, *op. cit.*, 95-6.

[2] One at least of the Serbian agents of Raguzinsky was a monk, Moses Mitoanovitch, who adoped the rank and name of Captain Ivan Ivanovich Albaneza; Bogoyavlensky, *loc. cit.*, 31. Among the Serbs and Montenegrins the church was identified with armed struggle and national resistance, in a way that was not the case with the Greek clergy of Constantinople and the towns, who were so closely linked with the Ottoman administration. Until the close of the seventeenth century Russian connections with the Orthodox in Turkey had been mainly with the least militant, and most urban, of the Orthodox, the Greeks, and with the Rumanians. In Peter's time there comes about a marked change. For Serbs priest and peasant and *haiduk* could much more easily be one and the same person.

father's merchant business and later transferred to Constantinople, where he did well as one of Ukraintsev's secret agents. Tolstoi was equally impressed with him. He was an able and fertile man with multitudinous links, and his commercial energy specially attracted Peter, who called him to Russia in 1702. He was back again in Turkey in 1705 working for the Russians for three years, but then returned to Russia and rose high in Peter's favour. The Turks wanted him back; wanted his head; they demanded that he be handed over (together with Cantemir) in the negotiations on the Pruth, but the Russians evaded the demand, and he lived on for many years in their service (he did not die till 1738), for long in Italy and later, under Catherine I, as special envoy to China.

This ingenious, versatile, over-optimistic descendant of Bosnian princes (for so he claimed to be) was the mainspring, from the Russian side, of Peter's attempt to raise the Balkan Christians in aid of him. Early in March 1711 Peter approved a proclamation, probably composed by Raguzinsky, in which the tsar came forward avowedly as the liberator of the Christians, Catholic as well as Orthodox. It called upon the Christians in Serbia, Slavonia, Macedonia, Bosnia and Herzegovina to join together with the Russians "to fight for faith and fatherland, for your honour and glory, for the freedom and liberty of yourselves and your descendants"; thus would "the descendants of the heathen Mahomet be driven out into their old fatherland, the Arabian sands and steppes".[1] Raguzinsky was busy with his agents organizing the distribution of the proclamation among the Serbs and Montenegrins, and he himself was with the advanced guard of the Russians when they entered Moldavia. His plans must have been hastily drawn, and there could have been little enough organization, but in the summer his bellows raised the flames in the western Balkans, notably in Montenegro.

[1] The text has been frequently printed, e.g. in Golikov, *op. cit.*, xii, 278-83, but, as Bogoyavlensky, *loc. cit.*, 31 shows, this and other Russian printed versions are probably drafts and do not correspond exactly with the final original text, correctly printed by Serbian historians. The following paragraphs on the rising in Montenegro and Serbia are mainly based on Bogoyavlensky's article, itself based on the Russian archives and Serbian printed materials, and on Rovinsky, see following note.

While the opening of Peter's reign marks an increase of direct connections between Russia and the Serbs, 1711 marks the first relations of consequence with Montenegro. There the energetic prince-bishop Daniel Petrovich had been ruling ever since the age of sixteen (1697).[1] He had succeeded in difficult enough circumstances. The Venetian successes elsewhere had not been accompanied by any corresponding increase of their influence in Montenegro or Herzegovina. On the contrary, in 1690 the Turks had burnt Cettinje and reimposed tribute. Daniel bided his time and then, at Christmastide 1702, reacted with a massacre of Moslems and Montenegrins in league with them. Their retaliation was unsuccessful, and in 1706 they suffered a heavy defeat. This Montenegrin success was only temporary and munitions were hard to come by, but the spirit of the Black Mountain was high. Daniel enthusiastically welcomed the agents of Raguzinsky, led by a fighting chieftain from Herzegovina, Michael Miloradović, and in company with his two brothers took the lead in raising rebellion.

The revolt flared up rapidly and by mid-June successes had been gained. It was claimed that there were twenty to thirty thousand up in arms, with ten thousand Montenegrins in addition. But admittedly they were extremely ill armed, and they had no artillery. Hence against the Turkish strongholds they could do nothing decisive, and did well to achieve investment. Further, there were inevitable dissensions.[2] Many villages hung back, or contributed no help. Some were hostile. Despite the efforts of Miloradović at organization the rebellion was sporadic. Although the Turks suffered one defeat as far afield as Nish, the effectiveness of the rebellion seems to have been confined to Montenegro and southern Herzegovina, fastnesses which the Turks had never been able to subdue. There could be no question at all of linking up with the Russians, far away in

[1] He was not consecrated bishop until he was twenty, by patriarch Arsenius in Southern Hungary: P. Rovinsky, *Chernogoriya v ego proshlom i nastoyashchem*, in *Sbornik otdyeleniya russkago yazyka i slovesmosti* (St. Petersburg; 1888, 1879 and 1901), 1888, xlv, 513.

[2] There was no support from the patriarch of Peć, himself probably of Greek origin and only just appointed; Hadrovics, *op. cit.*, 149.

Moldavia,[1] and there is no evidence of the Turks being forced to divert troops to the north-west. In any case they were amply strong enough to outnumber heavily and defeat the Russians, as the battle on the Pruth showed (19-21 July).

The defeat was a fatal blow, but at first Daniel did not believe the news; when confirmed he refused to believe that peace had been concluded. The Montenegrins were duped by the conduct of a Russian adventurer, Pavel Arkulei, a sailor in the Russian fleet, who was sent as a courier to the Russian agents in Venice.[2] He appropriated some funds and appeared in Montenegro professing to be a secret diplomatic official of Peter. He declared that Peter was about to renew fighting against the Turks and called on Daniel to continue the struggle, and that Miloradović was empowered to conclude a treaty in the name of the tsar. Thus came about what is usually described as the first treaty ever made between Russia and Montenegro (27 April, 1712). This almost certainly unauthorised document was probably the handi-work of Arkulei acting on his own. Highly suspicious in form and vague and loose in content, it involved not so much re-cognition of Russian suzerainty as repudiation of any other suzerainty, whether Turkish of Venetian.[3]

Though the final crushing of rebellion in the western Balkans was delayed, the issue was not in doubt after the Russian catas-trophe on the Pruth. Daniel himself beat off a Turkish attack in 1712, but he had to face an invasion in force in 1714 and to

[1] The tale that Brancovan stopped 19,000 Austrian Serbs from moving to support Peter in the Pruth campaign seems to be based only on Thomas Canta-cuzene's calumniations. Raguzinsky had sent agents to recruit and rouse the Austrian Serbs, but the Austrian authorities took steps to forestall any large move-ment. They probably received nothing but supplementary information from Bran-covan. Actually a small band of one hundred and fifty Austrian Serbs took part in the battle on the Pruth, and a few of them subsequently entered the Russian army. Bogoyavlensky, *loc. cit.*, 28-30; Uebersberger, *op. cit.*, 97.

[2] On Tolstoi's imprisonment in the Tower of the Seven Bastions, the centre of Russian intrigues in the Balkans was moved to Venice, whither was sent Tolstoi's agent Mathew Caretta as diplomatic representative; Krylova, *loc. cit.*, 272; Bogoya-vlensky, *loc. cit.*, 30.

[3] The treaty is accepted as genuine by Rovinsky, *op. cit.*, 524-26, without discussion. Bogoyavlensky, *loc. cit.*, 36, shows good reasons for holding that the treaty, signed by Miloradović in the name of the tsar, was not the work of the Russian foreign office or anyone accredited by it.

flee the country for a time. He made his way to Russia to discover at first hand Peter's future intentions. The treaty of
Adrianople proved conclusively that Peter was intent on the
Baltic and Achmet on the reconquest of the Morea. Daniel
returned with subsidies (and portraits of the tsar), and arrangements were made to settle some of the rebels in Russia on
favourable terms; but in effect the Montenegrins and Serbs had
to face the Turks as best they could. Austria, not Russia, was
about to play the role of the liberator in her war of 1716-18,
and the treaty of Passarowitz for twenty years won for her a
commanding position. None the less, Peter the Great had initiated
relations with Montenegro which were to continue close for
the next two hundred years, and had multiplied connections
with the Serbs which were to bear fruit in the middle decades
of the eighteenth century in large migrations of colonists to the
Dnieper steppes.

VII

TURKEY, THE VOLGA MOSLEMS AND THE COSSACKS.

PETER the Great's relations with the Ottoman empire had
three intertwined aspects, relations with the Ottoman government, with the other foreign powers, and with the Christian
subjects of the sultan. All contemporaries agreed in the potential danger that Russia represented as a magnet for the Orthodox,
and that too even after the complete failure of Peter's
1711 campaign showed that he had trusted too much to tendent-
ious reports and had no time for effective preparations in the
Balkans. Austria had something of the same advantages as regards
the Catholics in European Turkey, but these were far fewer than
the Orthodox. France, despite her important Catholic connections in the Levant, Palestine and some of the Aegean islands,
necessarily played a very different role. No other European
power could make such an appeal as Russia to the Balkan Chris-

tians. Yet, conversely, in no other European country but Russia were there Moslem subjects of the ruling power to which the Turks for their part might make appeal. Might the Kazan Tatars, the Bashkirs and other Moslem peoples under Russian rule be an offset to the Balkan Orthodox? In alliance with the Volga Moslems, or at least as an alternative to them, might the unruly dissident Cossacks on Russia's southern frontiers be used by Turkey as a counter against Russian expansion towards the Turkish preserve of the Black Sea?

In the long run the Volga Moslems certainly proved to be no such offset, but in the seventeenth and early eighteenth centuries the question may perhaps be debatable. Turkish sources must be tapped, and I am myself unfortunately unequipped with Turkish. It may, however, be of use to indicate what light the Russian evidence in print throws upon the problem. There is not much of it as far as I am aware, but judging from that little the connections of the Volga-Ural Moslems with Constantinople seem to have been of very secondary importance, and even those with the Crimean Tatars comparatively minor.

The Russian authorities kept a sharp eye for reports of coming and going between their Moslem subjects and the Crimea, the Kuban and Turkey, more especially of course during the all too frequent periods of revolt in the turbid Volga-Don region. During the Bashkir revolt of 1662-64 there were said to be plans in concert between the Bashkirs, the Kazan Tatars and the khan of the Crimea. But, beyond the riding off of envoys to the Crimea and at any rate one appeal to the Turkish pasha at Azov, nothing material took place. The fact that the Buddhist Kalmuks were in the main hostile to the Moslem Bashkirs and Tatars and gave information to Moscow added to the difficulties both of communication and of any combined action against the Russians. The Bashkirs were more drawn in fact eastwards, much nearer home, to the descendants of Kuchuk khan of the Siberian Tatars than to the far away khan of the Crimea or the still more distant sultan of Turkey.[1]

[1] Soloviev, *op. cit.*, xii, 576-77; N. V. Ustyugov, "Bashkirskoe vosstanie 1662-64 gg.", in *Istoricheskie Zapiski*, 1947, xxiv, 65-67; A. Chuloshnikov, *Materialy*

Nor did combined action take place in the early sixteen-seventies when the Volga Moslems were greatly stirred by the outbreak of Stenka Razin and the resultant wholesale Muscovite repression. A deputation of seven Bashkirs and Tatars from Kazan and Astrakhan appeared in Constantinople and Adrianople in 1672 asking for Turkish troops: then they would rise in arms and beat the Russians and put themselves under the Sultan. But there was no effective result.[1] Six years later another deputation from Kazan and Astrakhan made their way to the Crimea and were shepherded on to the sultan at Adrianople. The news of the Turkish success at Chigirin had spread to the Volga and inspired the Moslems to further hopes of aid in riddance of the Russian yoke. "We are of one family and spirit with them" (the Crimean Tatars and the Turks) the Bashkirs cried.[2] But again there seems to have been no material response; nothing but words and presents. It is perhaps significant that, when in 1675 a Russian expedition was being prepared against the Crimea, a levy was ordered from the Bashkirs. Some went: some refused, pleading various reasons:—there was no obligation to serve; they feared Kalmuk depredations while away, or trouble from the Siberian side; but there is no hint in the Russian reports that they would not serve against fellow Moslems whom they felt to be their potential liberators.[3]

A generation later Peter was faced with yet another Bashkir revolt against Russian penetration and oppression (1705-11). These were the most anxious years of his reign, when Charles XII

po istorii bashkirskoi A.S.S.R. (Moscow; 1936), i, 169. After 1683 the Kalmuks, under Ayuk Khan who ruled them with great effect until his death in 1723, were almost invariably in close league with the Russians against the various Tatar hordes and the Bashkirs, who greatly feared them. Peter the Great was careful to keep Ayuk well supplied with gifts. There is a first hand account of the visit of Peter and Catherine to Ayuk in 1722, on their way to Astrakhan for the campaign against Persia, in John Bell (one of Peter's Scottish doctors), *Travels from St. Petersburg in Russia to diverse parts of Asia* (Glasgow; 1763), ii, 331-34.

[1] N. A. Smirnov, *Rossiya i Turtsiya v XVI—XVII vv.* (Moscow; 1946), ii, 121, 122-23.

[2] Smirnov, *op. cit.*, ii, 162; Soloviev, *op. cit.*, xiii, 861. Presumably the Volga Moslems were also spurred on by a Turkish-Tatar attempt in 1677 against Astrakhan. There is an account of this in *Zapiski odesskago obshchestva istorii i drevnosti*, 1872, viii, "Istoriya o prikhod turetskago i tatarskago voinstva pod Astrakhanye v lyeto ot R. Khr. 1677", but I have not been able to consult a copy.

[3] Text of reports in Chuloshnikov, *op. cit.*, i, 198-205.

dominated Poland and was moving east against an isolated Russia, when Astrakhan flared up in rebellion, when Bulavin raised the Don country in a blaze, when Mazepa threw in his lot with Charles and the Zaporozhian Cossacks followed suit. The running sore of the Bashkir revolt added greatly to the strain, and at one moment (May—June, 1708) Peter, in fear of Azov and Taganrog falling into Bulavin's hands and perhaps of possible Turkish action, even made preparations to go south and deal with Bulavin himself.

Among the Bashkirs and in Kazan there was talk of Turkish assistance and of the Volga returning to its rightful owners, the Moslems. Much more dangerous; once again emissaries had been sent, via the Kuban and the Crimea, to Constantinople, though the Bashkirs were not united in seeking such aid, for many feared reprisals.[1] One steppe adventurer, Sultan Murat (he appears also as Sultan Ibrahim and Sultan Khozya), after making his way to the Bosphorus, returned to set alight the Tatars of the North Caucasus steppes and try to drive the Russians from the Terek. Prompt action was taken from Astrakhan. His band was routed and he himself captured and hung. His deposition after capture is interesting. It gives the impression that in the Crimea and Constantinople he was regarded at best as a useful, but minor, trouble maker, at worst as a roving adventurer out to pick up what he could. He seems to have received little serious encouragement from the Turks, and there is no mention of any links with mullahs or of the fanning of religious zeal.[2]

Much requires to be known from Turkish sources, especially as regards the attitude of the Ottoman government. Is there, for

[1] V. I. Lebedev, "Bashkirskoe vosstanie 1705-11 gg.", in *Istoricheskie Zapiski*, 1937, i, 87-88, 92. Sultan Murat rode south, making for the Kuban and the Crimea, with fifty of "the best Bashkirs": only he himself and eight others reached the Kuban: the remainder had fallen into the hands of the Kalmuks.

[2] On Sultan Murat: documents in *Pisma i Bumagi Petra Veligako*, iv, 452; v. 173; vi, 506; vii, pt. i, 208, 621; vii, pt. ii, 750-51; *Istoriya Tatarii v dokumentakh i materialakh* (Moscow; 1937) 391; Chuloshnikov, *op. cit.*, i, 225. His deposition is in Chuloshnikov, *op. cit.*, i, 238-43, and also in *Istoriya Tatarii ..·.*, 391-96. Sultan Murat according to his own account was not a Bashkir but a Karakalpak or Kirghiz, who after various adventures in the Volga-Yaik steppes came north to Bashkiria. He was captured in March 1708, just before Bulavin's capture of Cherkassk and threatened action against Azov and the despatch of his letter to the sultan of Turkey through the Kuban Tatars (see below).

instance, from the Moslem side anything corresponding to Peter's appeals to the Orthodox to rise in 1711 ? The Russian sources speak only of appeals to, not from, the Crimea and Constantinople. The scattered references which I have indicated suggest as a provisional verdict that the Moslems in Russia were less played upon as a disruptive threat than the Orthodox in the Balkans. They were, after all, more distant and more scattered. They were quite as much, if not more, divided among themselves. Their religious connections were probably closer with Bukhara and Central Asia than with Constantinople. Russian colonization was spreading around and amongst them whereas in the Balkans there was no similar extension of Moslem settlements. The most incitable region, most open to direct Turkish influence, and nearest geographically, the Kuban steppes, was in Peter's day still under nominal Turkish, not Russian, overlordship. The Kuban Tatars were a very real threat to the Russian Cossack outposts on the Terek and they were at constant loggerheads with the Don Cossacks, though as well with the Crimean Tatars. Peter's expansive designs along the Caspian and in the Caucasus in the last four years of his reign opened the long period of rivalry between Russia and Turkey for the mastery of the North Caucasus steppes, which was not finally settled in favour of Russia until the end of the eighteenth century. Since, however, in Peter's day the Kuban steppes were not yet engulphed in Russia, Turkish connections with the Tatars there are not comparable with Russian connections with the Orthodox in the Turkish dominions.

The Kuban Tatars figured at one critical moment as the possible allies (in conjunction with the Turks) of the dissident Cossacks and runaways who flocked to the standard of Bulavin in 1708, "the children of the arch-subtle devil".[1] When Bulavin seized Cherkassk and threatened Azov itself, he despatched envoys to the Kuban Tatars (7 June) with a long and involved letter to be sent to the sultan at Constantinople, calling on him to attack Azov; "and if our tsar will not make grants to us as he did to our fathers and grandfathers and forefathers . . . we will cut off the

[1] F. M. Apraxin's description of the Bulavin rebels; *Pisma i Bumagi* . . . , vii, pt. ii, 752.

Host [i.e. the Don Cossacks] from him and will àsk favours of
... the Turkish tsar, so that he does not reject us."[1] This vague
appeal in fact had no result, and Bulavin almost immediately
afterwards rode up northwards, but the idea of desertion to the
Moslems was not new in the Don country, at any rate as a threat
to extract better conditions from the Muscovite government, and
one of Bulavin's principal henchmen, Nekrasov, in the end
made off to the Kuban, and from thence to Constantinople.
Tolstoi was on his tracks there, and Peter demanded his handing
over; but he failed to secure him from the Turks, and for the
next ten years or so this stormy petrel appears in the southern
steppes raiding with the Tatars and stirring up trouble for Peter.[2]
In the main, as even the most anxious years 1711 to 1713 showed,[3]
the steppes under Turkish or Tatar control could be an asylum
for the desperate, and a source for picking up sustenance and
arms, but not a solid rallying ground for an organized offensive
northwards by Russian disruptive elements.

Nekrasov and his followers were the exception among the
Don Cossacks. The great bulk of "the Host" would not turn
to the Crimea or Turkey. A more likely weapon against Peter
might be the Zaporozhian Cossacks, who had never unequivocally
acknowledged Russian supremacy and who felt their liberties
threatened by Kamenny Zaton and other new outpost forts

[1] Text of letter in *Bulavinskoe Vosstanie* (Moscow; 1935), 461-65; Bulavin's ideas
of securing assistance from the Tatars and the Turks, or of taking refuge with the
Kuban Tatars, were known to Ivan Tolstoi, the governor of Azov; *ib.* 258, 269-70.

[2] *Ibidem*, 360; *Pisma i Bumagi* . . . , viii, pt. i, 378; *Sbornik* . . . , xxv, 373;
Golikov, *Dyeyaniya* . . . , xi supplement, 498-50; Elagin, *Istoriya russkago flota*;
Prilozheniya, ii, 374-5; Soloviev, *op. cit.*, xvi, 652. His followers remained for
a generation in the Kuban steppes, but during the war of 1735-39 were forced
to migrate and took refuge in the Dobrudja, still keeping the name of Nekrasovtsy.
Hammer-Purgstall; *Geschichte der Chane der Krim*, Vienna; 1856), 189, states
from Turkish sources that Kaplan-Girei, khan of the Crimea, was deposed,
in December 1707, because of a severe defeat by the Circassians and because
he settled "8,000 fugitive Cossacks from the rebellion of Ignatius" (Nekrasov).
This statement seems confused, since the rebellion was not at its height until 1708.
Soloviev, *op. cit.*, xv, 1470, mentions the figure of 2,000 rebels who made off with
Nekrasov to the Kuban in autumn in 1708.

[3] Early in 1711 Peter was evidently anxious as to the left-bank Ukraine: he
directs (3 Jan. 1711) prince Dimitri Mikhailovich Golitsyn, the governor of Kiev,
to watch carefully for any danger of "Ukrainian wavering" and to treat the hetman
Skoropadsky "cajolingly"; text in *Sbornik* . . . , xi, 93. In fact during the Pruth
campaign and the next few years no serious trouble arose in the left-bank Ukraine.

built by Peter. But their ataman Hordienko was no Sirko. As already mentioned, they joined Mazepa and Charles in 1709 and, despite some initial successes, suffered catastrophe in the destruction of the Sech by the Russians. The sultan held back the Crimean Khan and the attempt of Charles XII to combine Turkey, the Crimea, the Zaporozhian Cossacks and the Ukrainians in a grand alliance against the "Moskals" failed to materialize. The Zaporozhians took refuge under Crimean protection and were too few, too suspect, and too broken to serve as a leading element in any Turkish-Swedish drive northwards.

Probably the most dangerous dissident Cossack threat to the Russians came, not from the Don or Zaporozhian refugees, but from the little band of Mazepa's followers who had escaped with him and Charles XII after the defeat of Poltava. Though very few in numbers, they had a highly educated leader of determination, skill and experience in Philip Orlik, Mazepa's successor as émigré ataman. Orlik, like Rákóczy for Hungary, never wearied of building schemes for the rescue of the Ukraine, and he was hand in glove with Charles XII in urging the Turks to war against Russia. Later, and presumably at this time too (1710-13), Orlik pointed to the interest of Turkey in the Moslems "groaning under the yoke of Moscow" and pictured internal revolt in the great stretches between the Don and the Urals as the concomitant of an armed offensive of Turkey, the Crimea, Sweden and Poland which should press Peter the Great's Russia back into central Muscovy.[1] Whether the Turks believed in the likelihood of a revolt of the Volga Moslems I do not know, but no reference to them was made in the three war manifestos which they issued to their officials in 1710, 1711 and 1712.[2]

The threat to Russia, represented by Orlik, was minimized both by the fact that his own supporters, which included the Zaporozhian Cossacks, were few in number and short of money,

---

[1] E. Borshak, "Early Relations between England and Ukraine", in *Slavonic Review*, 1931, x, 153.

[2] Early December 1710, 17 December 1711, 20 November 1712; texts, in French, in W. Theyls, *Mémoires pour servir à l'histoire de Charles XII . . .* (Leyden; 1722), 7-13, 23-26, 63-66. The first manifesto was followed by actual war—the Pruth campaign: the other two were not.

and by the fact that his aims came into conflict now with those of Charles XII, now with the Poles, now with those of the Turks.[1]

Orlik succeeded in March 1712 in securing an agreement on paper with the Turks that he should be hetman of the unoccupied stretches of the right bank Dnieper and of the Zaporozhian Cossacks under Turkish protection. Such a return to the days of Hetman Doroshenko half a century earlier did not in actuality materialize. In any case, Orlik aimed ultimately at much more than this, at the reversion of all Ukrainian lands. He wanted the Polish Ukraine, at any rate the south-eastern part of it, and he wanted Kiev and the Russian Ukraine on the left bank of the Dnieper, whence he himself came. The former acquisition would have flung Poland into the arms of Russia, which was exactly what Turkish policy desired to avoid. The latter acquisition would have involved war to the bitter end with Russia, which only the most extreme "northerners" among the Turks were prepared seriously to contemplate. Charles XII, on the other hand, wanted just such a war, but he fell out with Orlik over the Polish Ukraine, for he could not abandon his puppet king Lesczyński.

No king of Poland, whether Lesczyński or Augustus, could make concessions in the Polish Ukraine without the gravest risks. Peter the Great saw this clearly and in the interests of his alliance with Augustus against Charles XII refused to commit himself too deeply in the debatable Polish borderlands, Earlier, Mazepa had urged him to support the revolt of the Cossack Paley against Polish rule (1699-1704), but Peter, although his troops both then and subsequently marched and countermarched almost at will through these regions, would not follow Mazepa's advice and join the Polish Cossack lands to Mazepa's Ukraine on the other side of the Dnieper.[2] Nor did he change his policy after Poltava. He held to his ally Augustus. After the Pruth and the loss of Azov Augustus did indeed have to pay a price to Peter, but the price was in the north not the south, the abandonment to Russia of the Polish claim to Livonia.

[1] For this and the following paragraphs on Orlik, see, besides Borshak, *loc. cit.*, B. Krupnyckyj, *Geschichte der Ukraine* (Leipzig; 1939), 152-59.
[2] Allen, *op. cit.*, 184-86; Soloviev, *op. cit.*, xv, 1284-86, 1288-89; Doroshenko, *op. cit.*, 376-80.

The tangled events of 1710-14 brought out clearly one main weakness of Orlik's position: he was almost as suspect to the Poles as he was to the Russians. Early in 1711, at the head of the Zaporozhian Cossacks, in company with the Crimean Tatars, he swept up into the right bank Ukraine, but he failed either to hamper seriously Russian military plans or to consolidate his position.[1] The Crimean Tatars proved the worst of allies and soon made off home after indiscriminate looting, but another main reason for his failure was inability to win the confidence of the Cossacks of the Polish Ukraine and to prevent dissensions with the Poles. It was the same story late in 1712 when he repeated his incursion and was defeated by the Poles.[2]

From the mizmaze of intrigues in Constantinople between Orlik, the Turks, the Crimean Tatars, Charles XII and the Poles (including at one moment Augustus II), with Shafirov and Tolstoi from the Tower of the Seven Bastions doing their utmost to prevent the Turks renewing the war,—from this mizmaze four results emerged, which removed the immediate menace of a Cossack-Turkish-Swedish-Polish combination against Russia.

(i) In March 1713 Devlet-Girei, the russophobe fire-eater, was deposed from the Crimean khanate.

(ii) In the end, the Pruth terms were sufficiently carried out by Peter to give the advantage to those Turkish politicians who regarded war with Venice and the reconquest of the Morea as the first essential and were opposed to elaborate and expensive combinations for a drive northward against Russia. Thus, in June 1713, the treaty of Adrianople reaffirmed the Pruth terms in respect of the cession of Azov and Taganrog and the abandonment of Kamenny Zaton and certain other Dnieper fortresses, the Zaporozhian Cossacks and any claims on the right bank of the Dnieper, save for Kiev. The Russian frontier was pushed back substantially to the river Orel.[3]

---

[1] Doroshenko, *op. cit.*, 400-402.
[2] Hrushevski, *A History of the Ukraine* (New Haven; 1937), 372.
[3] The text of the treaty of Adrianople is in Noradounghian, *op. cit.*, i, 203-07. It was substantially the same, save for two important points, as the abortive Russo-Turkish treaty of April 1712; text in Theyls, *op. cit.*, 46-56, in French, and *Reformy Petra I*, ed. by V. I. Lebedev (Moscow; 1937), 248-55, in Russian; the original

(iii) In April 1714 the Sultan concluded a treaty with Augustus II recognizing his possession of the Polish Ukraine. This marked the final discomfiture of Lesczyński's hopes of Turkish support, and a few months later he himself left Turkey, where he had taken refuge, for Hungary. It marked too the closing stage of the Turkish embroilment with Charles XII.

(iv) In February 1713 the Turks had lost all patience with the intractable—and extremely expensive—Charles. He was seized, after a violent struggle against impossible odds,[1] and removed from the Dniester frontier to semi-confinement near Adrianople. Next year, at long last the Turks were rid of him. In October, 1714, he started on the most dramatic ride in modern European history.

Thus Orlik lost his two most hopeful supporters, Charles and Devlet-Girei, and he lost any Turkish support for his far-flung designs on the Russians and Polish Ukraine. Peter had a firm peace with Turkey, and his Polish ally Augustus recognition by Constantinople. Orlik left Turkey for the West, to continue his projects for a coalition against Russia. In the end he failed in these and returned to Turkey, but he remained true to his conception of Ukrainian patriotism, and he came into prominence again, as adviser to the Turks, during the Russo-Turkish war of 1735-39. By then, however, he was deprived even of the backing of the Zaporozhian Cossacks. They had found conditions intolerable in their new abode by the Dnieper estuary under the protection of the Crimean Tatars, and in 1734 had transferred themselves to Russian suzerainty and returned to a new Sech further up the river. Orlik's hopes of using the war to regain a position in the

was in Russian (with an Italian translation) and Turkish. The two major points of difference concerned the Russian evacuation of Polish territory (a cardinal requirement of the Turks, as well as of Charles XII) and Charles's return to Sweden. The 1712 treaty provided for evacuation within three months; the 1713 treaty within two months. By the 1712 terms Charles might even return through Russia; by the 1713 terms only Poland was mentioned. In neither treaty did the Crimean khan gain any recognition of tribute from Russia.

[1] A new account of Charles's resistance—one of the most incredible among his many fantastic exploits—is given in the account by a French merchant in Bender at the time, printed from the Quai d'Orsay archives, by A. N. Kurat, *Izveç Kirali XII Karl 'in Türkiyede Kaldiği zamana ait metinler ve vesikalar* (Istanbul; 1943), pt. i, 187-92, in the original French.

Ukraine once again came to nothing.   He died at Jassy in 1742 after thirty-three years of unrelenting struggle in exile.

I have discussed the career of Orlik relatively at some length because the doings of unsuccessful émigrés are too apt to be treated by later historians as foredoomed to failure and therefore futile and unimportant.   Yet they are not so foredoomed, even though, as I have tried to show, the dissident Cossack threat to Russia had the scales heavily weighted against it.   It was a threat that caused Peter much anxiety, and more trouble than the threat of the Moslem appeal to Russian Moslems.

VIII

RUSSIAN DIPLOMATIC REPRESENTA-
TION AT CONSTANTINOPLE

THE reign of Peter the Great marks the beginning of regular Russian diplomatic representation in various European capitals.   The same right was won at Constantinople in 1700. Though lost in 1711, it was regained in 1720 and was never thereafter questioned.   This unexciting, prosaic fact was perhaps the most important outcome of Peter's relations with the Ottoman empire.   It gave Russia much better chances of information and influence and some possibility of direct action at Constantinople, and it put her on an equality with the other powers which had regularly resident envoys there,—France, the Empire, Great Britain, the Netherlands, and Venice.[1]

Throughout the seventeenth century an increasingly frequent succession of Russian envoys had made the toilsome, and frequently dangerous, journey from Moscow to Constantinople, usually down to Azov and then by sea in a Turkish ship, sometimes by the Crimea or the Principalities.   Turkish missions had

---

[1] Sweden did not have regularly resident ministers until 1745.   Poland, though her envoys to Constantinople were even more frequent than those of Russia in the seventeenth century, continued in the eighteenth century to be without regularly resident ministers there: B. Spuler, "Europäische Diplomaten in Konstantinopel biz zum . . . 1739", in *Jahrbücher für Geschichte Osteuropas*, 1936, i.

journeyed likewise to Moscow. These were despatched for particular purposes and made but a brief stay. For the first time during the Karlowitz negotiations the demand for a permanent mission was put forward by Voznitsyn, and it was successfully insisted upon by Ukraintsev and written into the treaty he negotiated in Constantinople in 1700.[1] These were the two men to whom Peter initially entrusted his relations with Turkey. They were both inherited by him as officials in the Moscow foreign office with long experience, particularly of Turkish affairs, trained under Ordin-Nashchokin and Matveyev to western contacts and ways. Ukraintsev appears to have been somewhat the older man; he was certainly the senior of the two in the civil service.[2] From 1665 onwards he appears on various special missions abroad, including two to Warsaw, and rose steadily, despite the political oscillations of 1676-89, to a commanding position in the foreign office. Both under Sofia and V. V. Golitsyn (1682-89) and during the next ten years he was the chief diplomatic expert of the government, especially in matters relating to Turkey, and he accompanied Golitsyn on both his Crimean campaigns.

Voznitsyn, whose ancestors had been dispossessed of their Novgorod lands by Ivan III and resettled in the Moscow region, came of a family that had long been connected with the civil service. Like Ukraintsev he had considerable experience of Warsaw, and in addition some knowledge of Constantinople, which he visited in 1681 to negotiate the conclusion of the treaty of Bakhchi-Sarai made with the khan of the Crimean Tatars. He did well, but on the overthrow of Sofia in 1689 he left the foreign office and attached himself to Boris Golitsyn at the head of the Kazan department. This was a turning point in his career, for Golitsyn was one of Peter's closest supporters and Voznitsyn became personally known to him. As a result Peter chose him

---

[1] Apparently without any difficulty, Bogoslovsky, *op. cit.*, v, has only one reference to the matter, 215-16.

[2] He served continuously in the *posolsky prikaz*; was made a *dyak* in 1673, *dumny dyak* in 1682, and *dumny sovyetnik* (a new title) in 1700. Voznitsyn was made a *dyak* in 1681, *dumny dyak* in 1690, and *dumny sovyetnik* in 1700. Details for both are in S. K. Bogoyavlensky, *Prikaznye sudi XVII vyeka* (Moscow; 1946). For Voznitsyn see also Bogoslovsky, *op. cit.*, iii, 342-43. Both are in the Brockhaus and Efron encyclopaedia; neither in the *Russky Biografichesky Slovar*.

as third envoy, together with Golovin and Lefort, to head the "grand embassy" on which Peter set out, nominally incognito, in 1697 to tour the West. In Vienna Peter left him in utmost haste, to patch up peace with the Turks (see above p. 19). Voznitsyn was unsuccessful; whether from his own lack of dexterity or from the difficulties of the position in which the Russians had been placed by the Austrians it is difficult to say. A two-year truce was all that he brought back. As has been seen earlier, a year and a half later Ukraintsev succeeded in Constantinople where Voznitsyn had failed at Karlowitz.

It took Ukraintsev, however, nine precious months to conclude his negotiations, months during which Peter was chafing to have his hands free for war with Sweden. For this long delay Ukraintsev seems to have been at least in part himself responsible, by his adherence to the traditional minutiae of Muscovite diplomatic usage and by his desire to win certain small gains which his master was willing to sacrifice.[1] Upon his return home at the end of 1700 he appears to have blackened the reputation of Voznitsyn, who disappears thereafter mysteriously unrecorded. Ukraintsev some years later fell into disfavour on bribery charges, but he was employed in important negotiations in Poland in 1707, and in the following year on a mission to Rákóczy in Hungary where he died (1708).

Very different were the careers and personalities of the four other men whom Peter employed at Constantinople, Tolstoi, Shafirov, Dashkov, and Nepluyev. All of them were made by Peter, Shafirov and Nepluyev entirely so, Tolstoi and Dashkov predominantly.

Petr Andreyevich Tolstoi (1645-1729) is the sole example of a man from a middling landed family who began as a supporter of Peter's opponents, the Miloslavsky and the Regent Sofia, and ended by becoming one of Peter's most powerful and trusted counsellors. He had changed on to Peter's side in 1689, but his new master did not trust him and sent him off to minor provincial

---

[1] Bogoslovsky, *op. cit.*, v. 247-49. The whole of this, the last volume of Bogoslovsky's detailed work, is devoted to Ukraintsev's mission in Constantinople.

administration.[1] He did well on the second Azov campaign and, though he was already over fifty, he showed that he was fully in tune with Peter's ideas and requirements by volunteering to learn navigation in Italy. There he learnt also to speak Italian very well, a useful asset when he was sent to Constantinople in 1701 as the first Russian minister there. When he returned to Russia thirteen years later, he was rewarded with high favours and a variety of difficult tasks, most notably that of luring the tsarevich Alexis back to Russia. This success set the seal on Peter's high estimation of him. He was made head of the secret chancellery and throughout the dark, closing years of the reign was one of the most powerful men in Petersburg, in close alliance with Catherine. In the end, but after Peter's death, he fell out with Menshikov on the succession question, and he died in exile in 1729 in the Solovetsky monastery. Cultivated and western inclined, eloquent and crafty, unscrupulous, sinister and vindictive, a man of cool head and deliberate action, Tolstoi was a determined character of very varied talents and experience, well suited to play the part of Russia's first representative on the Bosphorus with great effect.

He began under the greatest difficulties, being even more confined to his legation quarters than the other foreign representatives in theirs. None the less he succeeded in building up a very fair information service, that owed much in the first instance to the old Russian henchman Dositheus, patriarch of Jerusalem. He had been patriarch ever since 1669, rarely in Jerusalem itself, and not once since 1690, spending his time for the most part in Constantinople or the Principalities. His nephew and successor (1707) Chrysanthus was a principal intermediary. To the all important chief dragoman Alexander Mavrocordato he was long well known. Dositheus continued intermittently in direct correspondence with Peter, who paid him well, and Tolstoi valued

---

[1] He was voivod of Ustyug in 1694, when he entertained Peter on his way to Arkhangel; Bogoslovsky, *op. cit.*, i, 179. Perhaps he made a strong impression on Peter then, but his reconciliation probably also owed something—possibly much—to the fact that he was related to Apraxin, one of Peter's most influential favourites; Soloviev, *op. cit.*, xiv, 1329.

him highly: "truly, despising the fear of death, he works for the Lord Sovereign on all occasions".[1]

From the first, however, Tolstoi began to weave additional connections through other sources than Greek ecclesiastics. The able, ambitious Dalmatian merchant Sava Raguzinsky served him well (see above p. 46), and through him relations were es-- tablished with the French embassy.[2] Others from the Illyrian lands were enlisted, including two active Catholic ecclesiastics, Gallani and Zmaevsky, whose brother became an admiral in the Russian navy (see above p. 19, note). Zmaevsky, a Slav from Ragusa and at one time archbishop of Cattaro, had a hand in stirring up the Serbs and Montenegrins to revolt.[3] Gallani, a Dominican and apostolic delegate at Constantinople, played something of the same role, but he was in and out on all sides, in the pay now of the Russians, now of the French, now of the Austrians: in the end Russia did not pay well enough and he withdrew to Ragusa as bishop.[4]

Among the non-Orthodox, however, probably the most effective assistance was given to Tolstoi and his successors by the Dutch resident Jacobus Coljer and his dragoman William Theyls. The other foreign missions varied in their attitude, according to the chops and changes of policy, but the Dutch were continuously, until 1719, a mainstay for the Russians in the intricacies of Turkish politics and court vagaries. Coljer knew the ground thoroughly from thirty years' experience, first under his father and then since 1684 in succession to him as resident.[5]

Much work is needed on the details of Russian diplomacy at Constantinople during Peter's reign before a clear picture can be drawn of Russian sources of information and means of influence; nevertheless one generalization may be hazarded. Tolstoi seems

---

[1] Report of Tolstoi, 14 June, 1703, text in *Pisma i Bumagi* . . . , ii, 228. There are letters to and from Dositheus and Peter, 1701, 1702 and 1704, *ibidem*, i, 470-73, ii, 341-49, 715-21.

[2] Krylova, *loc. cit.*, 263.

[3] Bogoyavlensky, in *Voprosy istorii*, *loc. cit.*, 28.

[4] *Ibidem*, 40; C. Scheffer, *Mémoire sur l'ambassade de France à Constantinople* . . . (Paris; 1894), xxiii; Hurmuzaki, *Fragmente* . . . , iv, 203, 264; Spuler, in *Jahrbücher für Kultur und Geschichte der Slaven*, 1935, xi, 205.

[5] Spuler, in *Jahrbücher für Geschichte Osteuropas*, i, 1936, 258-59.

to have increasingly veered away from the previous Russian practice of reliance almost entirely on the Greeks of the Phanar. The patriarchs of Constantinople, who in any case had always had to use the utmost caution in devious communications with the Russians, appear to have had scarcely any connections with him or his successors. Shortly after Chrysanthus succeeded his uncle Dositheus as patriarch of Jerusalem in 1707, a pronounced change set in. For the first year or two Chrysanthus, in the Principalities, continued in close relations with the Russians,[1] but by 1711 he was suspected of double dealing and though connections were not severed until 1713, thereafter they were never resumed until 1728, and then only through the Synod on non-political matters.[2] This may be perhaps symptomatic of a turning away from the Greeks on the part of the Russians.

In general, the religious and cultural links between the two, which had been steadily increasing during the first three-quarters of the seventeenth century, had declined in the last quarter, when Kiev not Constantinople proved itself the leading Orthodox cultural influence on Russia. When in 1685-86 the metropolitan-ate of Kiev was placed under the jurisdiction of the Moscow patriarchate, this was effected without previous agreement with Constantinople, and the patriarch could do nothing but register unavailing protests.[3] Ukrainians, not Greeks, became the leading representatives in Russia of new trends in Orthodox thought and education. Constantinople no longer as in the days of Nikon represented for Russia the fountainhead of learning and of Or-thodox tradition.[4] Thus, even apart from the ardent westernism of Peter (which was openly and boldly denounced by Dositheus

---

[1] *Pisma i Bumagi* . . . , v, 630-33; vii, pt. i, 114, 466-87.

[2] Kapterev, *Snosheniya* . . . , 374-417. Soloviev, *op. cit.*, xvi, 88, cites a report of Shafirov in 1712 stating that an additional count against Chrysanthus was the fact that he had been appointed "Cossack patriarch", but he does not give any particulars as to the exact meaning of this.

[3] Kapterev, *Kharakhter* . . . , 460-67; *Snosheniya* . . . , 252-66.

[4] Very few high Greek ecclesiastics received posts from Peter in Russia, and these few reinforced the decline in Greek prestige; e.g. the bishop of Smolensk (formerly Philotheus, archbishop of Okhrida) and Athanasius Kondoili, archpriest of Vologda, who quarrelled, intrigued, and did nothing for education; Kapterev, *Kharakhter* . . . , 475. In 1721, when the Holy Synod was set up, the name of the patriarch of Constantinople was omitted from prayers in Russia; *ib.*, 473.

and by the patriarch of Constantinople), the general prestige of the Greeks had heavily declined by the beginning of the eighteenth century To Peter himself and his supporters the Greeks counted for little or nothing beyond the political help they might be able to bring. This seems to have been the attitude of Tolstoi and his successors at Constantinople, who were strong westerners and had no sentimental or traditional feelings in favour of Greek Orthodoxy.

After Peter's defeat on the Pruth, when Shafirov and Tolstoi were hostages in the hands of the Turks and their stars at their lowest, they required all possible help. None came from the Greeks in Constantinople (save for one faithful henchman, Luke Kirikov[1]). Tolstoi unburdened himself:—"In truth, from small to great, they all lie and it is utterly impossible to trust them". Shafirov denounced them in unmeasured terms: "for money they are ready to sell—their God, their faith, their soul, and their sovereign": their information "must be weighed on diamond scales": among them is not to be found "either a friend or a good man": in difficult times "they fly from the foreign diplomats as from the plague".[2] That was but natural, and the Russian tirades against the Greeks of the Phanar cannot be taken at their face value. Yet it probably remains true that from about this time dates a long standing break between the Russian legation and the ecclesiastical hierarchy and the Greek effendi class in Constantinople and the Principalities, where from the time of the Pruth campaign they displaced Roumanians as hospodars for over a century.

These years of seesaw balancing between peace and war

[1] Soloviev, *op. cit.*, xvi, 85.

[2] Kapterev, *Snosheniya* . . . , 413. Ten years later (1723), Nepluyev reported bitterly on the patriarch of Constantinople as having no use for the Russians; *ib*. Vyeshnyakov, his successor at Constantinople, lashed out against the Phanariot Greeks as being, for the most part, "idlers, without faith or law or honour, serving only their own interests, our enemies, worse than the Turks themselves" (report of 25 April, 1736). He contrasted them with the up country Greeks, Bulgars and Rumanians, who looked to Russia and were prepared to make sacrifices in throwing off the Turkish yoke. A. A. Kochubinsky, *Graf Osterman i razdyel Turtsii*, 141. The fact was that most of the well to do Phanariot Greeks were by this time far too closely connected with the administration of the empire (including particularly the Principalities) to have any sympathy with Russian dreams of a rising of the Christians and a drastic reduction in Turkish power in the Balkans.

(1711-13) brought Shafirov to Turkey virtually as a hostage, to negotiate the ratification and carrying out of the Pruth terms. Shafirov (1669-1739), twenty-five years younger than Tolstoi, was completely different both in origin and character. He was one of those low born protégés, like Menshikov and Yaguzhinsky, whom Peter raised from nothing to great influence, thereby exacerbating feelings against the new regime. He belonged to a family of converted Jews in the Smolensk region. His father served as a translator in the foreign office, and he himself, after various small commercial dealings, worked his way up from the same post in the foreign office (1691) to become one of Peter's principal diplomatic lieutenants. He made himself indispensable through his excellent knowledge of western languages, including Latin, and his great ability at drafting. Fat and comfortable, with a broad smile and fertile in resource, he knew how to make his way, first with Ukraintsev, then with Golovin, whom he accompanied on the "grand embassy" to the West in 1697-98, finally with Peter himself. On Golovin's death in 1706, his place as foreign minister was taken by Golovkin, another boyar who was equally a convinced westerner but was a man of very different character and of less attainments. Shafirov at first throve under him, but they fell apart and a long period of bitter rivalry set in. In 1711, Shafirov, by then a secret counsellor and vice-chancellor, was taken by Peter on the Pruth campaign as head of his diplomatic chancellery. Hence it fell to him to secure from the grand vizier the peace terms that rescued Peter from his disastrous predicament. It remained to secure from the Sultan their ratification—a still more intricate task.

He did not begin too well and had to be overruled by Peter, perhaps because Shafirov himself at first was at Adrianople and not yet in touch with Tolstoi, who was still confined in the Tower of the Seven Bastions in Constantinople, and therefore could not assist with his local knowledge and experience of the Turks.[1] Shafirov was handicapped not only by the swiftly changing vortex of politics and intrigue around the sultan, but by the ex-

---

[1] The fullest account from the side of the Russians of their negotiations with Turkey, 1711-13, is still that of Soloviev, *op. cit.*, xvi, 75-99.

treme slowness of communications with Russia,[1] the obstinacy of Peter, and the hostility of Golovkin, who was accused by Shafirov of leaving him on purpose in the lurch. Under the circumstances, however, it was inevitable that Shafirov and Tolstoi had largely to fend for themselves. When direct negotiations broke down and war again was imminent, both of them suffered renewed confinement by the Turks and they became mainly dependent on the unwearying efforts of the Dutch and British ministers to counter French and Swedish intrigues and to establish a firm peace between Russia and Turkey.[2]

Peter, once his army was saved and was marching back to the Dnieper, adopted the line that his fulfilment of the Pruth terms was dependent on the departure of Charles XII from Turkey. Hence he delayed handing over Azov and Taganrog. The Turks insisted on the Pruth terms being carried out whether or no arrangements could be made for the departure of Charles. Peter was left in no doubt of this by the reports of Shafirov and by information from Sheremeteyev in command in the Ukraine.[3] In mid-November, 1711, Peter gave in, but before the news of this concession reached Constantinople the war party had gained the day and it was only in February 1712 that the Turks were convinced of the abandonment of Azov and Taganrog and deferred

[1] Peter himself went to Carlsbad to take the waters in the autumn of 1711 and was thereafter in Germany and did not return to Russia until January 1712. From June 1712 till April 1713 he was again away in Pomerania and on the Baltic coast. These instances involved still slower communications with Constantinople.

[2] As already mentioned, the despatches of Sutton are to be published in a forthcoming volume of the Camden series by Professor A. N. Kurat, the leading Turkish authority on Russo-Turkish relations at this time. Their publication should throw a flood of light on the exceptionally tangled course of events, particularly from the Turkish standpoint, which is probably the main key to a full understanding of the negotiations with the Russians. From the Dutch side there is much information (including documents) in W. Theyls, *Mémoires pour servir à l'histoire de Charles XII* ... (Leyden; 1722). Theyls was the dragoman of Coljer, the Dutch resident, and was the intermediary of Shafirov.

[3] The alarms and excursions over the carrying out of the Pruth treaty are well illustrated in Sheremeteyev's papers, printed in *Sbornik* ..., xxv. When early in November 1711 Mehemet Pasha was replaced as grand vizier by the bellicose Yusuf Pasha, and Devlet Girei, the Swedes and Orlik had succeeded in heading the Turks to a resumption of war, Shafirov, though he had previously counselled the giving up of Azov, boldly advised that it be retained, since now it seemed that in any case war would begin in the spring of 1712: reports to Sheremeteyev, 21 and 24 November, texts in *ib.*, 341-44.

hostilities. The remaining Pruth terms—Russian evacuation of Poland and of the Dnieper fortresses, non-intervention with the Cossacks—and the burning question of Charles XII gave ample opportunities for the warmongers at Constantinople to frustrate Shafirov's efforts to make a firm peace with the Turks.

Hence, though he gained a marked success in April, 1712, by concluding a treaty, with indescribable "hurry and confusion",[1] which substantially repeated that of the previous year (see above p. 57, n. 3), it proved abortive; for the Turks, egged on by the French, were now more than ever insistent on complete Russian evacuation of Poland, a measure which in view of Russian operations in Swedish Pomerania and their lines of communication through Polish territory it was in any case almost impossible to carry out. Again, as in the previous autumn, it came to the brink of war. A high Turkish functionary had been sent to Poland to make enquiries on the spot and had returned (via Bender where he was inspired by Charles XII and Devlet-Girei with their war plans) bringing information that there were still many Russian troops in Poland.[2] Yusuf gave place as grand vizier to Suleiman Pasha, a pliant son-in-law of the sultan, and in November, 1712 another war manifesto was issued and Shafirov and his company were again immured in the Tower of the Seven Bastions.

Shafirov met this second crisis with the same bravery and dexterity as before, and spared no means of keeping in secret, devious touch with Sutton and Coljer, the reis-effendi and the mufti. Peter refused to be browbeaten by the demands of the Porte, or to be intimidated by heavy raids by the Crimean Tatars, with the renegade Don Cossack, Nekrasov, in their company.[3] The firmness of the Russians reacted to the sharp discomfiture of the war party in Constantinople and Bender. Akhmet III felt himself duped, and he broke both with Charles XII and with

---

[1] Despatch of Sutton, 7 April (O.S.), in *P.R.O., S.P.*, 97/22: the negotiations were in the hands of the Sultan and grand vizier alone: Devlet-Girei was at this moment in the Crimea.

[2] Text of report of Talmann (Constantinople) to Vienna, 18 November, 1712, in A. N. Kurat, *op. cit.*, 180-84; Soloviev, *op. cit.*, xvi, 91.

[3] *Sbornik* . . . , xxv, 375, text of letter of Sheremeteyev, 2 April, 1713.

Devlet-Girei (*cf.* above pp. 57-8).   In February, 1713, Shafirov was able to restart indirect negotiations which after five months of kaleidoscopic veerings and heavy bribing resulted at long last in a definitive peace, the treaty of Adrianople.   He had to agree to Russian evacuation of Poland within two months and to the frontier in the Ukraine being pushed northwards between the rivers Samara and Orel, but he held out successfully against a belated but most dangerous requirement of the Turks that they should settle the Zaporozhian Cossacks under their protection along this nebulous frontier.[1]

To the very end the Crimean Tatars persisted in their demand for the renewal of annual tribute.[2]   As has been pointed out earlier, this had been explicitly repudiated by Peter in the treaty of 1700,[3] and the Pruth treaty, by making no mention of this thorny claim, left the matter open.   Now the insistence of the Crimean khan almost wrecked agreement.   Under threat of personal danger, Shafirov was at one moment induced by Mavrocordato to promise 120,000 rixdalers to the khan "for the abandonment of all his claims": this was little enough in comparison with the khan's demand for an annual tribute of 80,000 rixdalers, but in the end Kaplan-Girei over-reached himself.[4]   The reis-effendi, and the mufti, heavily bribed by the Russians, stood out for a settlement with Shafirov.   The Turks needed to have their hands free for revenge against Venice and the reconquest of the Morea.   Hence the Adrianople terms, like those signed on the Pruth, omitted all question of tribute to the Crimea.

The terms were ratified without delay, but the Turks would not allow Shafirov to depart until they were duly carried out, and it was not until September, 1714, that he and Tolstoi finally set out for Russia.

---

[1] Theyls, *op. cit.*, 94, 98; Soloviev, *op. cit.*, xvi, 97-98.

[2] Efforts had been made by Golovkin a year earlier, June, 1712, to come to a direct deal with the Crimean khan, then Devlet-Girei, and to buy him off with an extra large gift of the usual sort, namely furs, but nothing had been achieved; instructions to Sheremeteyev, text in *Sbornik . . .* , xxv, 360-64.

[3] This question had proved one of the most difficult in Ukraintsev's negotiations in Constantinople in 1700, as is shown in Bogoslovsky, *op. cit.*, v, 78, 211-12, 144-49, 155-57, 162-63, 193.

[4] Theyls, *op. cit.*, 98, 112-13; report of Fleischmann (Constantinople) to Vienna, 26 May, 1713, text in Kurat, *op. cit.*, 213, mentioning 30,000 ducats.

The resource and the courage that Shafirov had displayed in Turkey earned him his master's full approbation. For the next ten years he was one of Peter's right hand men in foreign affairs, and at the same time an active manipulator of commercial and manufacturing projects. His fertile ingenuity in trade and industry was just what Peter wanted from his chief servants, and what he found in far too few of them. He was prepared to overlook much in return for inventiveness, drive, and optimism. In the end Shafirov went too far. He had risen from nothing to great power and great wealth, and, though he had married his four beautiful daughters into four of the highest families in Russia, he was widely regarded as a crooked upstart and he had only too many enemies. Like so many of Peter's ministers and administrators—but unlike his enemy Golovkin who remained his nominal chief at the head of the foreign office and unlike Osterman who became his rival in diplomacy—he enmeshed himself in embezzlement and bribery and came to grief in the scandals of 1723 when he was cashiered for the rest of the reign. Later he made his way back, and once again played a prominent part in Turkish affairs under Empress Anna.

When Shafirov and Tolstoi left Turkey in 1714, there was no successor as Russian minister. The Pruth terms held good, and the right to permanent representation at Constantinople was not regained. This was a major object for Peter. For the next few years the Turks rebuffed Peter's envoys and he had to make do with Coljer in his pay as unofficial Russian agent. The victories of Austria and the treaty of Passarowitz altered the political scene, and gave Peter the opportunity to press effectively for concessions to Russia as an offset. In May 1719 Dashkov arrived in Constantinople charged with far-reaching proposals.

The contrast between Dashkov and Shafirov was as complete as that between Shafirov and Tolstoi. The Dashkovs, reputedly descended from a refugee from the Horde in the early sixteenth century, were a wealthy landowning family, though none had risen high in service of the state. Alexis Ivanovich Dashkov (d. 1733) had begun as a youth with an appointment at the court of the tsaritsa Praskovya Saltykova, the wife of Peter's half-brother Ivan V. This in itself was in his favour, for Peter's relations with his sister-in-law were always friendly, but Dashkov did not begin seriously to make his way until he went with Matveyev on his mission to the Hague in 1699. He imbibed western education, knowing both Latin and German, and he learnt much from being attached to Patkul at the court of Augustus II (1704). Two further spells of diplomacy in Poland, as resident to the grand crown hetman (1708-12, 1715-16), gave him good experience, but he does not appear to have made any special mark. If Austrian accounts are reliable, he had indeed fallen into Peter's disfavour, but recovered it in 1718 by being the first Russian to discover the plan for the marriage of the Austrian archduchess Maria Josepha, daughter of Joseph I, to the son and heir of Augustus II of Saxony and Poland.[1]

This marriage alliance was part and parcel of the ambitious combination initiated by George I, that was being woven to frustrate Russia by a coalition of Great Britain-Hanover, the Empire, Sweden and Saxony-Poland. Augustus was to be encouraged by hopes both of a hereditary throne in Warsaw and of support for his schemes for making royal power in Poland a reality; the Poles themselves were to be won over by hopes of regaining the lands they had lost to Russia, even perhaps Smolensk and Kiev. Dashkov was despatched to Constantinople to use the levers of the overgreat power of Austria and of the mutual danger of a strong, revived Poland to re-establish a Russian legation there. As earlier, Constantinople reflected the European struggle for power and the final clashes of the Great Northern War were echoed on the Bosphorus.

Dashkov, outrivalling the pomp and hauteur of the Austrian internuncio, played a bold hand, aided only by de Bonnac, the French minister. This assistance, however, was of great importance, for de Bonnac had excellent connections with the innermost circles through the sultan's Jewish doctor Fonseca.[2] Had French support not been forthcoming, Dashkov would have been badly placed. The British, in contrast with their attitude

[1] Hurmuzaki, *Fragmente* . . . , iv. 193.
[2] *ib.*, 230.

during the years 1710-13, were now leagued with the Austrians in opposition to Russia.[1] The Dutch, as Dashkov bitterly complained, were useless. Coljer was by this time senile and incompetent. Theyls did little effective for the Russians, and his son Nicholas, who had succeeded him as dragoman, was hand in glove with the Austrians.[2]

Dashkov succeeded in alarming the Turks with his news of the Austro-Polish marriage agreement and of the prospect of Austrian predominance in a greatly strengthened Poland. As already noted (see above, p. 35, n. 4), he made much of the Russian refusal of overtures from Vienna and Venice to join in the recent war against Turkey. He suggested an offensive and defensive alliance, asked that no objection be raised to the entry of Russian troops into Poland,[3] put forward Rákóczy as a rival to Augustus for the throne of Poland, and insisted that the situation required a regular resident Russian minister at Constantinople.[4]

In addition, the old demands were put forward that the Tatar khan should not claim annual tribute and that Russian merchants should be granted freedom to trade by land and sea throughout the whole empire.[5]

The Austrians were greatly perturbed by the intrigues with Rákóczy and won a marked success when in April 1720, he was banished to Rodosto. That proved to be much too near Constantinople to prevent a continuation of far-flung Russian and

---

[1] The despatches of Stanyan, British minister in Constantinople, in P.R.O., S.P. 97/24, contain a good deal of information (particularly 12 February (O.S.) and 2 March (O.S.), 1720) on his fruitless efforts in combination with Virmont, the Austrian minister, to defeat Dashkov by contriving a Swedish-Turkish alliance. He complained much of lack of money and authority to bribe, and he failed to secure any audience with the grand vizier before Dashkov's treaty was signed. By the end of March the utmost that he hoped to achieve was "clogging" Dashkov's treaty "with some article in favour of Sweden". He did not succeed even in this. The position of Sweden, he complained, was much weakened by the fact that she still had no envoy accredited at Constantinople.

[2] Hurmuzaki, op. cit., 263; Soloviev, op. cit., xvii, 591-92.

[3] All Russian troops had been withdrawn from Poland by 1719, but the revolt of the four Polish-Lithuanian hetmans against Flemming and Augustus's schemes for Saxon domination opened the door for a return of Russian influence and troops.

[4] Hurmuzaki, op. cit., 194-96; Soloviev, op. cit., xvii, 591.

[5] P.R.O., S.P., 97/24; "principal points demanded" by Dashkov; an unsigned, undated, document in French following Stanyan's despatch of 19 August (O.S.), 1720. Dashkov secured in his treaty freedom of trade by land, but not by sea.

French projects for countering the anti-Russian combination by aiding Hungarian and Jacobite exiles. Ultimately, nothing effectual was accomplished. Rákóczy never went either to Poland as king or to Hungary to raise insurrection again; nor did the Old Pretender set foot once more in Scotland.[1]

These were minor issues for the Russians, intended only as one form of counter attack against British and Austrian projects. The main task of the Dashkov mission was to prevent any Turkish intervention on behalf of Sweden and to counter the effect on the Turks of Austria's triumph at Passarowitz by assurances of Russian amity and by the restoration of permanent representation at Constantinople. After protracted negotiations Dashkov achieved this last object by the treaty of Constantinople signed in November 1720.[2]

The peace between the two countries was declared to be permanent, whereas that of 1713 had been for twenty-five years only. In addition, Russia gained the restoration of the article in the treaty of 1700 providing for freedom of pilgrimage to the Holy Land. Once again the inevitable struggle over tribute to the Crimean Tatars was long drawn out and hotly contested. Once again, Peter remained obdurate and the treaty was silent as to this perennial claim. An involved article on Poland gave fair scope for continued Russian intervention. Given the general situation, Dashkov may be said to have scored a success.

The following year the Great Northern War was at last concluded. The treaty of Nystad (1721) sealed the Russian victory over Sweden. Peter's hands were free on the South, and he at once launched out with unsparing energy against Persia in Trans-Caucasia, where inevitably he soon became involved again with Turkey. It did not fall to Dashkov to keep Russia clear of another war in the dangerous and involved negotiations that dragged on at Constantinople during the next four years.[3] That was the task of his successor Neplyuev.

[1] Hurmuzaki, *op. cit.*, 230, 238, 252-56.
[2] *Ibidem*, 239-49. The text is in Noradounghian, *op. cit.*, i, 227-33.
[3] Thereafter Dashkov played no conspicuous role, although he married one of Menshikov's daughters. Peter made him general director of posts. He was on the side of the "oligarchs" in 1730, but none the less was made a secret counsellor in that year.

Ivan Ivanovich Nepluyev (1693-1773), the last of Peter's representatives at Constantinople, was a young man after Peter's heart. Together with Tatishchev he is perhaps the best known of Peter's "fledgelings", and like him was later to play a great part in Bashkiria as governor-general of Orenburg. He owed everything to Peter, was a whole-hearted admirer, and spared nothing in his service. To him Peter was in very truth the "father of his country", and his tears and oft-quoted encomium when the masterful emperor died were entirely genuine. Yet in origin he came from the camp of Peter's opponents. Nepluyev belonged to an old, highly connected middling landowner family in the Novgorod region, closely linked to Old Believers and antagonists of Peter's westernized ways. While himself remaining strictly Orthodox and deeply earnest, the conservative, anti-western impress of his early years did not long survive his entry into service. In 1714 he was sent to the Novgorod "cipher" school, and then to the Narva navigation school, whence he was transferred to another of Peter's favourite new establishments, the St. Petersburg naval academy. From there he was sent abroad for five years of naval instruction, and he served some time in the Venetian fleet against the Turks. On return he was for a brief spell put in charge of shipbuilding in St. Petersburg. There his efficient probity and attractive manliness won Peter's personal favour, and he was appointed Russian resident in Constantinople (1721).

It remains difficult to explain why Peter should thus have wasted so much naval training and appointed a man without any diplomatic experience to so important a centre as Constantinople. His knowledge of Italian was his only specific asset for the post. His youth (he was only twenty-eight) would have been no disqualification. Volynsky had been picked by Peter for his highly successful mission to Persia at the same age, and was promoted to the governorship of Astrakhan when only thirty. In any case, the choice was a good one. Nepluyev toiled unweariedly at Constantinople for thirteen years and it was in great part due to his pertinacity, hard work, and good relations with the French mission that war with Turkey over Persia and the

Causasus was avoided and a *modus vivendi* reached that satisfied Peter's chief object—to keep the Turks from the Caspian.[1]

This final, Caucasian period of Peter's relations with the Ottoman Empire must be left for a later study. All that can be said here is to emphasize again that the Asiatic rivalry of the two countries is not much less important than the far better known and more prominent clash in the Balkans, and that the Armenians and Georgians figure from Peter's time onwards as the eastern counterparts of the Serbs and Montenegrins. We must leave Nepluyev settling down at Buyuk-Dere. After some years he brought his wife there, the first Russian to do so. This detail may be taken as a symbol. Another power, the harshly westernized Russia, was also beginning to make herself at home on the Bosphorus.

IX

GAINS AND LOSSES: THE OLD AND THE NEW

PETER the Great's relations with the Ottoman Empire were direct and continuous to an extent that was new in Russian history. It was now no longer so predominantly a question of Turkey being involved as the suzerain of the Crimean Tatars. A new stage was marked by the war of 1676-81 between Russia and Turkey, immediately before Peter's accession to the throne. This direct clash of the two countries was caused in part indeed by the Crimea, but mainly by the problem of the Cossacks on the right bank of the Dnieper. The advance of Russia to Kiev and the left bank of the Dnieper, at the immediate expense of Poland, meant both that Russian power and prestige were increased and that there was now a third magnet for the remainder of the Ukraine, those great tracts between the Dnieper and the Dniester which ever since the days of Vitovt had swayed between Lithuania, Poland, the Cossacks, the Crimea and Turkey.

Peter inherited this new aspect of the Ukrainian problem.

---

[1] For Nepluyev's early life, V. N. Vitevsky, *I. I. Nepluyev i Orenburgsky krai ... do 1758 g.*, (Kazan; 1889), i, 17-49.

He inherited likewise the new approach that took definite shape with the treaty of 1686 between Russia and Poland, whereby Poland abandoned definitively all claims to Kiev and Russia in return bound herself to active alliance against Turkey. The immediate results were Golitsyn's two disastrous campaigns against the Crimea and a state of war against Turkey. Thus, Russia in alliance with Poland was linked with Poland's other two allies Austria and Venice. It was the first appearance of Russia alongside of, though not technically a member of, an European coalition. Peter moved a step forward when he concluded in 1697 the first Russian alliance with Austria, for three years, against Turkey. It did not run half its course. Austria made her peace at Karlowitz to free her hands for the West (1698). Peter, regarding himself as deserted, never forgave Austria and remained on the worst possible terms with her until the very end of his reign, when a change set in culminating in the alliance with Vienna signed in 1726, the year after his death, which lasted (with all too many rubs) until the close of the Seven Years' War.

Such were the two novel inheritances of Peter, when in 1695 he took power unto himself. As of old he had the problem of the Crimean Tatars,—raids, Russian prisoners in their hands and sold in Turkish slave marts, annual tribute. As of old the Zaporozhian Cossacks, by the Dnieper cataracts, and the Don Cossacks, shut off from the sea by the commanding Turkish fortress of Azov, made for perpetual frontier friction.

What did Peter attempt? what did he claim? what did he accomplish?

While continuing the policy of war in the South in conjunction with the triple alliance against Turkey, he adopted means that were new to Russia,—direct attack on Azov (1695, 1696), which was captured at the second attempt, combined with the creation of a fleet. He forced the Turks to agree to the cession of Azov by the treaty of 1700. Despite the immense cost in human labour and expenditure, he pushed on with the building of his fleet and the creation of a new port at Taganrog. All this was lost and wasted when in 1711 as a result of the disaster on the Pruth he had to retrocede the acquisitions of 1700. They were partially regained in 1739, but not fully until 1774.

Kerch, the key to the entrance of the Sea of Azov and hence the prerequisite for a Russian Black Sea fleet based on Taganrog, was demanded in the negotiations carried on by Voznitsyn (1698) and by Ukraintsev (1700), but the claim was abandoned by Peter in imperative need of peace with Turkey in order to fight Sweden, and he was never thereafter in a position to renew the claim. Kerch fell to the Russians only when Catherine II incorporated the Crimea in 1783.

The claim to freedom of navigation of the Black Sea, a consequential part of Peter's Azov-fleet policy and linked with his demands for a commercial treaty, was put forward for the first time by Voznitsyn and was renewed by Ukraintsev and Tolstoi unsuccessfully. Freedom of navigation was not acknowledged by Turkey until 1774, and the first Russo-Turkish commercial treaty was not signed until 1783.

These temporary acquisitions and these claims broke new ground. At the same time, Peter followed old lines by thrusting down the Dnieper with notable success (1695). The Turks had to give ground, and the Zaporozhian Cossacks were brought more effectively into the Russian sphere of influence. All the advantages gained in 1700 had to be abandoned in 1711, when Peter was forced back to his original frontier, the river Orel. By the treaty of Belgrade (1739) what was lost by him was substantially regained.

The payment of annual tribute to the Crimean Tatars was repudiated by Peter.[1] The treaty of 1700 (and that of 1709) included Turkish recognition of this repudiation. The article in question did not reappear in any of Peter's subsequent treaties, but he stuck successfully to his guns in refusing the obdurate demands of the khan for recognition of annual tribute. The question was left in the air by the treaties of 1711, 1712, 1713 and 1720.

---

[1] It had not been paid since 1683. According to Ukraintsev's calculations the amount owing for the years 1684—1699 was 237,020 roubles; Bogoslovsky, *op. cit.*, v, 145. Peter's annual revenue was about 1,500,000 roubles in 1684, but by 1701 was nearly 3,000,000 roubles.

For the first time in Russian history claims were officially put forward on behalf of the Orthodox in the Ottoman empire, and, when it came to the war of 1711, for the first time Russia adopted the overt policy of appealing to the Balkan Christians to rise against their Turkish masters. In addition, freedom for Russian pilgrimage to the Holy Land, which had figured in earlier negotiations, was successfully insisted upon in 1700, and, though this right was lost in 1711, it was regained in 1720.

The claims on behalf of the Orthodox in the Ottoman empire were twofold. In the first place, they concerned the controversy over the Holy Places between the Greeks and the Latins. Voznitsyn, Ukraintsev and Tolstoi all put forward demands for the handing over of the Holy Sepulchre to the Greeks. They failed. In the second place, a general guarantee of freedom of religion for the Orthodox figured in the negotiations both of 1698 and 1700, though without result. It was not obtained until 1774.

The Pruth campaign in 1711 was signalized by the two novelties of Peter's appeals to the Balkan Christians and by his striking direct for the Principalities and the Danube. Both of these novelties were to become commonplaces in Russian policy for the next hundred and fifty years. Cantemir of Moldavia, though not Brancovan of Wallachia, joined Peter at the last moment in alliance, but his limited aid was quite insufficient to prevent the Russian disaster on the Pruth. Only in Montenegro and parts of Serbia did a rising of the Christians take place, fanned by Peter's emissaries. It achieved nothing. Nevertheless, with Peter began continuous direct relations with the Montenegrins and with the Serbs (mainly in southern Hungary). A few of these latter took service with Russia, a harbinger of the Serbian colonists in south Russia under Elizabeth and Catherine II. Peter the Great was far from forgotten in the Balkans, despite his military defeat. Russia had stood out for the first time openly as the champion in arms of the Orthodox against the Moslems— and against the Catholics.

Finally, in this summary of Peter's gains and losses, there is his one important lasting acquisition for Russia—permanent diplomatic representation at Constantinople, which put her on a footing of equality with the other European powers. It was demanded for the first time by Peter, conceded by the Turks in 1700, withdrawn in 1711, but again conceded in 1720, and never again questioned.

If the Caucasus had been included in this sketch, some compensation for Peter's setbacks would have been found in his success in barring to the Turks expansion to the Caspian and in his temporary acquisition of the Caspian littoral provinces of Persia. When he died in 1725, these were the only territorial acquisitions on the south which he retained. Within ten years his successors handed them back to Persia, but Turkey did not penetrate to the Caspian. Further, if Peter's relations with the Georgians and Armenians had been treated here, it would have been shown that these relations, already in the seventeenth century steadily increasing in frequency, were assiduously strengthened and for a time at the close of his reign were more prominent than Russian links with the Orthodox in the Balkans.

Surveying Peter's reign as a whole, there is no doubt that he accomplished little against Turkey, in striking contrast with the achievements of Austria. One explanation of the contrast lies in the fact that Austria and Turkey were contiguous, whereas Russia and Turkey as yet were not really so. The settled regions of the two empires were still separated, though the gap was slowly closing, by the debatable steppe lands, across which neither power could strike sustainedly.

It may be argued that the Turkish victory on the Pruth was more decisive in immediate results than the Russian victory of Poltava. Russia gave up at once all that had been gained eleven years before. Sweden did not finally give in until twelve years later. The protracted complications of the Great Northern War and the immense strain of the ultimately successful struggle for the Baltic were the essential reasons why Peter failed against Turkey. If he had devoted the labour and energy he poured out on St. Petersburg instead to colonization and the pushing out of defence lines in the South, if his military reorganization and re-armament had been carried out primarily with an eye to the conditions of steppe warfare, the tale might perhaps have been different. He might have retained and strengthened his southern fleet, and his Black Sea dreams possibly might have been sooner realized. Such concentration on the South was not possible at one and the same time as concentration on the West. The South, relatively speaking, was abandoned for the West. The Baltic replaced the Black Sea in Peter's vision of the immediate task before him; for the Baltic (in which was summed up victory over Sweden and the triumph of his new capital St. Petersburg) was in his eyes the necessary means towards the fulfilment of that task, namely, the refashioning of the Muscovite tsardom into the Russian empire through close and unimpeded contact with the West. By 1725 this transformation was well under way, and, despite the vicissitudes and vagaries of Peter's successors, it was not seriously halted. No transformation comparable in magnitude took place in the Ottoman empire. By 1725 the balance of real power between the two empires was tilted in Russia's favour, and thereafter Peter's legacy was slowly and fitfully fulfilled.

Merezhkovsky's trilogy on Julian the Apostate, Leonardo da Vinci and Peter the Great has as the sub-title of the second novel "the Forerunner" and as that of the third "Anti-Christ". Peter was indeed to many of his subjects Anti-Christ, but in much he was also the Forerunner, not least in his relations with the Ottoman empire.

DATE DUE

5/22/70			
NOV 25 1970			
AU 14 '82			
OC 2 '85			
GAYLORD			PRINTED IN U.S.A